May you also
experience things
are with the One !

Emily

one
with the
One

How Suffering Taught
That We are Eternal
and are Loved

EMILY JEAN ENTWISTLE

BALBOA.PRESS
A DIVISION OF HAY HOUSE

Balboa Press books may be ordered through booksellers or by contacting:

Balboa Press
A Division of Hay House
1663 Liberty Drive
Bloomington, IN 47403
www.balboapress.com
844-682-1282

Print information available on the last page.

ISBN: 978-1-9822-5075-1 (sc)
ISBN: 978-1-9822-5077-5 (hc)
ISBN: 978-1-9822-5076-8 (e)

Library of Congress Control Number: 2020918583

Balboa Press rev. date: 03/19/2021

Words do not teach at all. It is life experiences that brings you your knowing. But when you hear words that are a vibrational match to the knowing that you have accumulated, then sometimes it's easier for you to sort it all out.

Esther Hicks (Abraham and Jerry) excerpted from Chicago IL on 11/2/97

Contents

PART III: REFLECTIONS FOR YOU

*To the Jonathans, the first was my teacher
and the second, my sweet reward.*

Introduction

2020

A small town in Northern Arizona

TODAY, I FEEL JOYFUL AND FREE. All the suffering I felt before this, I now see as beneficial. Through experience and grace, I've learned the truth: *My mind creates*. It can morph my reality into joy or sorrow, and what I think and feel in this moment, if I persist in the feeling, predicts my future. I know this, too: *I have free will, and this was given to me out of love*. I wasn't born into a life of love. Nor was I born knowing how to use my will. I suspect that most people learn through trial and error, or not at all. What I have learned I will happily share with you here.

I've found that working with my beliefs changes my life. But there is a method to this: A right way and a wrong way that wasn't explained in any sort of training manual issued to me as a little girl. How about you? Did you get the "Little Book of Rules" and it's only me that didn't? All I know from experience is that trying to willfully fix a problem that develops out of my own negativity and fear, or sense of victimhood, is like trying to unravel a ball of yarn that's been tossed around for years. Who can find the end? Who can undo the knots now pulled so tight? So here's my own personal truth on how to fix something I don't like about my life: *Define, in my own mind, my positive future reality, and then live as if it is already true.* I don't use my will to change outward circumstances. I use my will to see only what I wish to see in my mind's eye, as if all the negative outward conditions do not exist.

I'm not a philosopher, but rather a practical person who wants only to know how to live in happiness. Suffice it to say that certain philosophers and spiritual masters teach this, but I didn't know it until I learned on my own through inner direction and direct experience. I wouldn't have asked for inner direction and wouldn't have received the direct experiences if I hadn't sought God above all else. That's also what this book is about.

I've been taught by God through direct communion that I am an eternal being who creates. I know beyond doubt that I shall forever float in a vast sea of love, regardless of temporary outward appearances that my little self thinks and feels to be hard or sad or frightening.

I had inklings of this as a child, but didn't learn it was true until I died and went to heaven! There is a difference between taking something on faith and actual experience, a difference between trusting in someone else's opinion, and knowledge based on doing. And since I learned these differences, it hasn't been the same for me. What, from outward appearances looks like a lifetime of catastrophic events, is in fact a string of pearls blessing me beyond measure.

This might be a good time to tell you that I died and then came back to life again after a brain stem stroke. This is something that very few survive with the capacity that I now have. Not to say that I'm normal. I have right brain qualities that make my thought processes unlike yours, and a perspective on eternity that comes from my awareness of "the other side" or heaven.

I still tend to see, in my mind's eye, groupings of related information rather than a linear sequence of events. Over the years I tried to write this for you, my viewpoint repeatedly shifted, as onion rings of emotions peeled away, and the tug of war between my right and left brain became apparent to me. Pushing through fatigue and brain fog for decades after my return to a body, I felt compelled to create this for you in spite of my handicaps.

It is only in hindsight that I can see how far I've come in my ability to tell my story in a way that will be clear enough for most to follow. This healing work was done by my Higher, better self, rather than my little egoic self, and is evidence of grace, not will. However, criticize me, not God, if my story-telling falls short. God is perfect whereas I am a work in progress.

I know I must release this work of mine now, even if flawed. May I ask you to think of this as a candid revelation from a friend who hopes this will bring blessings to you?

Others like you have asked me to unfold this true story in the form of a "before" and "after." I said, "No, I don't want to relive the pain and confusion for I run the risk of putting myself in that treacherous frame of mind again. Why must I do that?"

Why, indeed. . . Because of the contrast it presents. I invite you to consider the transformative series of events that led me from discomfort and disconnection to the bliss of reunion---direct connection---with Our Source. I'm not going to limit this true story to "what" but expand it to "why" and "how," so that if you choose to imitate aspects of it yourself, you will know enough to get started.

I'll be describing my shift from separation to unity. I was quite lost, and then was found. Twice. The first time, I was catapulted into unity by my death. The second time, I sought unity by choice, having once again encountered defeat and despair when acting without divine help.

I died and left my body for Heaven, when forty-three years of age. I returned to physical reality with the mission of being a companion and nurse to my husband. The glow of Heaven remained for seven years after my return from heaven, but then the immediacy of my union with the One dulled and I felt pain and separation once again. After this, I trudged along using my will to persist against losing odds, until once again my body was dying when still needed as a care giver.

It wasn't through efforts of will, but by grace that I now live in a Heaven on Earth as I've always craved. I was taught directly, through surrender and intense listening and practice, the way to do this.

Let me explain a bit about how life began for me, for this will yield insights into the mindset I had when Part I of this story begins.

I was adopted by violent sexual predators at the age of six months. My adoptive mom and dad told me they'd taken me out of an orphanage where I'd been held from birth.

I knew nothing more of my roots until receiving a note while in my forties. It had been jotted down by an orphanage caseworker who'd interviewed my birth mother during intake at the Expectant Mothers Home. It gave only her first name. My father's name was omitted. Mother was, by her account, a Sunday School teacher, a secretary and a talented seamstress. The social worker noted that mother was tight-lipped and defiant. A psychologist wrote further, "No, just strong willed." As you'll read in my own story, this acorn, if I can refer to myself in this way, didn't fall far from the tree.

Per the note, I have a sister a few years older than me. I'll never find her, for my identity was changed when I disappeared into my new household, and her last name is unknown. Also noted, my birth mother planned to marry someone, not my father, as soon as I was born and gone. She left my half-sister with relatives, I imagine, while she hid away in the mothers quarters of the orphanage awaiting my birth. Perhaps my grandmother and aunts or uncles were drawn into her secret, keeping silent for the sake of her future.

It's fair to assume I would have been a deal breaker with her future husband. Can you, for a moment, imagine the stress and anger and fear in which I was steeped as I floated in the center of this, a tiny seed of life growing within the womb of a woman who would only be happy when I was disposed of?

My birth certificate obscures my true roots. Per this record, the couple who adopted me is falsely named as my birth mother and birth father.

No one involved in the adoption process seemed to know that the couple I was given to would not be good parents. When my adoptive mother died of dementia while I myself was in my fifties, I inherited letters from her estate regarding home visits, interviews with their friends and relatives, inquiries to their pastor and their doctor, and even lab tests to prove that they were fit. I wonder if, to this day, there is an effective screen to catch predators before they are given a child?

As noted, before I was placed into this couple's home, I'd lived my first six months of life in crowded quarters, caged in a metal barred bassinet with a lid. I know that we babies were crying with little comfort, because I was taken back to the orphanage and my little eyes and ears took it all in---the noise, the expanse of cage-like cribs, and the absence of caregivers. We went, mom, dad, and me, to pick up my adoptive brother, and I was taken into the heart of the institution before we left the facility with him. Then I was told that if I did not behave, I'd be returned to that barren place.

I was three years old when told this, my brain still wobbling between Delta and Theta waves and the entire world a dream, while my understanding of the world was being shaped by all the influences surrounding me, rather than my own logic.

I have a journal written by my adoptive father. According to the daily reportage, all in CAPITAL letters, I was constantly sick with temperatures, vomiting, and rashes. Over twenty courses of antibiotics were given before I began walking. I had surgery for lazy eyes when I was six and glasses for nearsightedness at age seven. I had a lisp treated by a speech therapist in my first two years of elementary school.

Outward appearances indicated that my physical needs were met, but I lived in fear and the bodily insults were hidden by clothing.

I've inherited photos, in shades of gray and sepia, now cracked and yellowing on the edges, fragile from time. In them, I see a vivacious two-year-old, full of life and joy. As if to belie this, I see another photo from the same time, in which I look stunned and sad. From that point forward, the pictures capture a withdrawn child with protective posture, hunching in on herself, not wishing to be viewed in all of her vulnerability by the photographer, as if forced to submit against her will by someone off scene.

When I had counseling in my twenties, the social worker said I had the attributes of someone abused as a child. Shockingly, she felt I'd been so abused that she thought I'd been used as an infant, continuing into my toddler years, in cult activities.

I had only vague recollections of the details of this. Yet, I had inexplicable damage to my body, and scars in my most intimate parts that I could not otherwise explain. What to make of this? I had all the feelings of abuse if not the memories. The memories seemed stored away in my flesh rather than in my brain.

Was I overly imaginative regarding possible abuse, succumbing to suggestion now? Or was I too frightened to recall? Maybe even programmed not to recall?

I vividly recalled the abuse my little brother received. He was often beaten, naked, in the basement, with a rubber hose. I could hear it as I stood frozen in fear at the top of the stairs. I saw it before I pressed the near-useless lock on the door handle of my bedroom, the only act I could take to secure my safety in such moments.

Once when he was twelve, he was locked into his room for days for some irrational reason by my mother. Agonized by this, I tried to help the only way I knew. The across-the-street neighbor saw me when I stood outside the house lifting the screen away to let him escape. Reported to my mother, I was punished. I can't recall the specifics of my own punishment to this day. Its okay if I don't unlock this memory even for you, isn't it?

I used my tape recorder when my brother was next attacked, to lend proof to his screams and pleas. I took this to a school counselor but only stony silence ensued. I tried to protect my brother, but could not. He bore this abuse, and as an adult was to say we had wonderful and loving parents. This made me feel even more disconnected from reality.

Until I applied special psychological techniques to unlock my memories decades later when stable enough for this, I remained without feelings about the abuse I myself suffered. I had only a pastiche of papers and perceptions to substantiate this, and if true, it was so unacceptable that I blocked many, but not all, of the memories out.

Many, but not all, of those involved are now passed away. In case of doing accidental harm to anyone perhaps still alive, some of the names and locations of my story have been changed to protect them. As for myself, I rest, ensconced in love from both the people now in my life, and by our Source. The sadness is over for me, and I pray the sadness is over for all others I shall be speaking of.

We'll pick up my story when in my mid-thirties, in Chapter 1. For the moment, forget about the fear and abandonment of my childhood. I made a life for myself, without looking back, and had a degree of success at this before a tragic event that was to take away most everything.

For as you'll learn more of in the chapters ahead, after I died of a stroke at age forty-three, all outward signs of success were stripped from me for decades to follow.

I left my body during a Code Blue, and spent an illuminating and blissful period of time on the other side, reunited with our Source. Then, I returned from the other side out of love for another. I was to live for decades more, under the specter of death from the blood cancer that was the cause of the stroke. I lived this way, stripped also of the love of family, physical and financial security, and of my freedom.

Physically and mentally disabled myself, I was by necessity the caregiver for the person I had returned from Heaven for. After thirteen years of caring for him, I learned I would not last much longer, and he would then be defenseless and alone. I did not want to see this happen to him.

With hope gone, I sought a direct experience of God once again. Words diminish the intensity of my seeking. I wanted to again know in my body, what I'd known on the other side.

Led by the still, small voice of my Higher Self, and with unending synchronicities, I then experienced what some have described as a miraculous healing of body, mind and soul. By this time, however, I knew that no miracle had occurred, and that my healing resulted from a glimmer of understanding of the laws of the Universe, coupled with my wholehearted willingness to change. It didn't happen overnight. It took more than two years to complete, four years to obtain irrefutable proof of healing, and I lost my loved one to death a few years after this.

My story illustrates how total healing of mind, body and spirit occurred. It illustrates, in my living of it, how I know that we are eternal and that we are loved beyond anyone's ability to define this.

It is my desire that someone, perhaps you, will read this when you are seeking new information and hoping for change. It is for those who at this moment have ears to hear, and those who will remember this and turn to it later, when ready.

This is an eternal tale, although played out in modern times with modern tools and techniques. Although it is a tale I believe is true, were I to jump into this same stream a decade from now, I expect that I'd tell it differently because of my growing beyond my present understanding. Both of us, you and I, perceive all things through our unique internal filters, our own vantage point, our own experience, and time changes all we think we know.

It is how we perceive ourselves and our life experiences in this moment that matters as we continue to create our future. I've come to believe that we exist both here and in a place outside of time and space, and from that perspective of eternity in which all events occur at once yet paradoxically are discrete moments, we can see that all turns out well and the rest are little adjustments required to make the incomplete, complete.

Let me put this concept in another way.

Imagine you are in the dark, and a candle burns before you. As your eyes adjust, there are many details you may observe in the candlelight, while it flickers to illuminate all that surrounds you.

How do you interpret what you see in the shadows? Now it is this, but in a moment it may be something else, as you shift in position, or the light flickers stronger, then weaker. As your eyes adjust to the darkness, you begin to see more.

For me, having come back from Heaven and all else that I've lived, the only unchanging truth is the light of the flame, imbued with the inherent love and goodness of its Maker, the ALL THAT IS, the Source and Its imaginings, thou and Thou. For we are one with the One, whether we know it at this moment, or not.

I

WORKING WITH
AFTER EFFECTS

The weeds will not be gathered and burned until the harvest comes.
(to summarize Jesus' parable of Matthew 13:24-30)

I BELIEVE THAT MY LIFE has a clear demarcation point: A before and an after. This epiphany opened me to grace. Before the epiphany, I thought life circumstances sprang up outside of me as random events. Do you ever think this way?

Being willful, I exerted myself to control outcomes in my life. I thought the results were subject to the impartial whimsy of harsh reality, and resented this. I tried to get better at controlling outcomes by developing my logic. Some might say I became more cunning and forceful.

What follows in Part One, "Working with After Effects," is a description of the events and emotions of those days. It led to my death in Intensive Care with a non-physical journey back to our spiritual Home, or what I often will call here, Heaven. When I returned to my body, I could not move or speak. After this, I swayed between my recollections of the beauty of the other side, and the hardships of this Earthly side of existence. I was eventually to face death again, at a time that would leave my loved one with no one to care for him through his own serious illness and dementia.

Here we are now, in my mid-thirties during my seemingly successful years. . . It was then that my soul agreed to the unimaginable in order to grow.

How It Appeared at the Time

1995
A small beach town in Southern California

I WAS MARRIED. I HAD BEEN SO FOR TWELVE YEARS. My husband intrigued me and occupied my mind and my heart, although we were long past the honeymoon stage. Former military, he had a mysterious past. Before we met, he had slipped back into the relaxed productivity of the West Coast as a telecom executive within a Fortune 100 company. He had a veneer of worldliness, polished by decades of life overseas.

How shall I describe our comingling?

He was not easy. Perhaps he carried secrets that haunted him, but his intense anger at these memories turned outward toward me, and I accepted it. In those times when I feared him, I made it a practice to *act* unperturbed, for this made me safer. This playacting would eventually seduce me into genuine feelings of kindness and forgiveness toward him once again.

Over and over, I moved in and out with this poisonous tide—wash me in and I crash on the rocks, wash me out and I feel human kindness well up within myself once again. And then I would forget that the rocks awaited me on the inevitable wash back to shore.

Yes, I loved him, but our marriage was sometimes difficult.

We shared a home on a hilltop looking down over the Pacific Ocean, in a sleepy beach town in Southern California. Prior to our marriage, I'd overcome my childhood shyness and fears, and was myself, a successful businesswoman. Financially independent through my diligent efforts, I believed that the world was a treacherous place, but that knowing this I could protect myself. Jonathan and I thought similarly about this. We were competitive people in a competitive world, and enjoyed sharing the rewards of our success.

We chose not to have children together, and set a plan to retire early and travel the world. I had studied psychology and knew that *if* I'd been abused as a child, I might perpetuate this. I was relieved that my husband was satisfied with two kids from a prior marriage, so that I would never have to find out if I might do harm to a child due to the irrational resurfacing of old patterns.

My work required meeting with decision makers in the Fortune 500 arena. I felt privileged to partner with bright individuals, both peers and clients, as I moved within these leadership and academic circles.

Advancing into positions of greater responsibility every few years, the high school diploma I'd earned at sixteen worked only so far. Motivated by the desire for further career advancement, I'd retired all but a handful of credits for concurrent Bachelors and Masters Degrees. A time saver was to skip the classes and go only for the final exams. Even though lacking diplomas, I was a guest lecturer at university level, teaching the technology I'd learned by doing.

Through my determination, I had created a fulfilling life. If my husband, Jonathan, and I seemed distant and sometimes disagreed, this was still acceptable compared to the example of marriage my adoptive parents had presented. On the whole, I thought things were going well for us.

Was the success I'm describing real? True? I ask this now, for underlying this veneer of what seemed to be success as I approached middle age, I feared I was damaged. I was thinking: *Can I always protect myself? Can I trust and love others now, when I couldn't as a child? Do I have discernment about what is good for me?*

I wondered why I had chosen a life partner as damaged as me. Was this why we were attracted to one another? We were like two waifs who had come in from cold and harsh isolation, now sharing with each other what little we felt safe to share at all.

Back then, even thinking about such things led to the anxious feeling I might lose control, and to lose control was to lose all I had worked for.

Better to be practical, and think of it like this: My husband, like me, had moved on from difficult beginnings and, so I thought, a secret past. Yet, he chose me as his companion, as I had chosen him. We were all alone in the world, yet we had each other to share what we were capable of, and in daily life we were a team.

He treated me as an equal partner in this marriage, for I could bring a great deal of wealth to our household, and, together since the 1980s, my income was a gift that kept on growing.

We had fun, I admit. When we were not working, we found time for weeks away in the Caribbean or central Mexico, and when unable to travel far, there was always our cabin cruiser to escape to for weekend jaunts over the waters of the Pacific. We both circled out over the country doing our work, but flew back like homing pigeons to our hilltop nest overlooking the sea, where we would settle into gliders on the back deck and watch the sun go down over the glistening waters rolling in to shore below us.

And so, I had "made it," as we've heard it said. Yet there was that fear in the back of my mind, pulsing with every heartbeat above my tightened gut, which seldom went away.

I am an empath, sensing the physical and emotional feelings of those around me. I had not yet learned, as I know today, how to parse my own feelings from those around me. My childhood environment had heightened this natural tendency, and this remained uncontrolled.

Being clairsentient had advantages, however. Sensing the feelings around me, it was only natural I often could quell the unspoken objections raised in business, and clear away misunderstandings. I could sense, as sweet as a sip of latte, when we were on the cusp of harmony and agreement and the mutual satisfaction that was always my goal. I sensed it when this overlap between others' energies and mine took place, and in this state it was possible to conclude that there was a Oneness to existence.

Yes, I was sensing something that was much different than I'd been taught during my Protestant upbringing. Was this Oneness

I sensed what others have called God? I had a somewhat defiant knowing or sensing about this — I knew that I was correct about this Oneness, this energy that encompassed all I might see or encounter in my reality, because this became palpable when in harmonious intersections with others. I also felt this in the quiet of my bedroom when the light peculiar to the Southern California coast shined in great pinkish swaths on the floor as I sat looking out at the ocean. This "presence" was not something that I thought should be prayed to, or to humble oneself before, however. I acknowledged its presence, but knew not what to "do" with it other than use it to improve my control of things. It didn't cross my mind to surrender to it, and it gave me no bliss or sense of connection to something glorious or caring.

To get back to the sensing of others' feelings due to the invisible threads connecting me to them, this wasn't always a helpful thing to me. Like a sponge, I absorbed everything, to include others' vibrations of anger, fear, and more. I didn't usually know why I felt drained or scattered. Zinging with the vibrations all around me, I felt emotions and sensations of all sorts. Had I been able to discharge this, it would have been wise to have done so, but I didn't know better then. Instead, because I had experienced how much pain one person could inflict upon another, I chose to retain all the anger, fear, and more, rather than harm anyone. I was a virtual maelstrom of emotion, ever-building without an outlet, and as a businesswoman in a world dominated by men, I had long since learned not to cry.

Pressure built further when my work hours extended to perhaps sixty-five a week. I had my corporate job, plus two side businesses, you see. I'd made it up the rungs of the ladder pretty well, and now dangled at the Regional Manager level, although given V.P. level responsibilities as a test. Not happy, I was always thinking ahead: *What do I need to do next to protect my position? How might this or that person or circumstance endanger or thwart me?*

7

Even worse, although outward appearances didn't give me away, I had a secret: I felt I was an imposter, and that if anyone found out who I was, I would lose everything. I needed the material security and my symbiotic relationship with Jonathan, or I would simply implode from fright.

In time, I tried to hold myself together through psychological counseling and prescription sedatives.

Counseling sessions had led me into a rabbit hole. I entered treatment with the belief that my internal foe, the cause of

> For God's Kingdom dwells in your heart and all around you; when you know your Self, you too shall be known. You'll be aware that you're the sons and daughters of our Living Father. But if you fail to know your own Self you're in hardship and are that hardship. (From the Gospel of Thomas translated by Alan Jacob)

panic attacks, was a fear of fear itself. How could it be true, as the psychologist suggested after months of sessions, that the origin of my fear was childhood abuse?

I didn't remember the earliest sexual attacks, but couldn't deny there was scar tissue gnarled deep inside me that had ripped and bled for days following each act of sex in early adulthood. It didn't stop until nine months after I thought I'd lost my virginity, in all subsequent acts of lovemaking that followed this supposed first event. Forced by the evidence, I accepted an M.D.'s opinion that early violence had occurred and my supposed hymen was nothing but torturously scarred flesh.

I *did* remember efforts to block my door and to hide beneath heavy blankets hoping I'd become invisible. I remembered nightmarish dreams of violation, but were they cover memories for acts of violence and loss of control? This was so, said my psychologist, when there were no other conclusions she could draw. *Okay*, I conceded, what I had recalled as nightmares were cover memories, meant to protect my sanity from what was too frightening to integrate into my conscious awareness. I'd fled my childhood home the day I'd turned eighteen and intended never to look back.

And so how was I seeing life in the rare moments when I was honest with myself, during that time in my late thirties in the midst of success and prosperity?

Fragile and tenuous. Programmed to believe that I wasn't worth loving, and that I wasn't competent or capable of success. Like I was imitating life as I thought it should be, as best as I was able, but it wasn't good enough. Like I was alone and defenseless against even myself.

I felt like a trapeze artist suspended in a pool of light illuminating my swing above the hushed crowd as the floodlights matched my moves through the air. There was no net beneath me. I feared the fall.

So there I was, settled into a marriage of compromise with Jonathan, projecting an outward appearance that hid my inner feelings, and it was at this point that my physical health unraveled. Before I became aware of this, something that I'll call "the agreement" occurred.

❦

The Agreement

1995

THE BREEZE CAME IN OFF THE PACIFIC, easing up the hill and entering the opened window of the bathroom as I finished applying my make-up. The room was lit by sunshine glinting over glossy white walls, glancing off the marble countertop, flashing rainbow rays from the beveled glass of the mirror. Just outside of the window, new shoots from my eucalyptus tree rustled their papery leaves toward me.

I looked at my reflection, and something indefinable shifted. It was as though time stopped. The pliable tree branches ceased to move, as I locked my gaze upon my own visage. Looking at myself, was that a stranger looking back at me? Like Earthly portals to the beyond, I saw deeply into the blue irises of my eyes, and past them, and I *felt* more than *heard* a question being posed to me. It said, "Are you ready? Do you still wish to proceed?"

11

I responded from that yet unknown place within me, "Yes, let it begin." With my answer, I felt energy shift from my heart to my solar plexus, realizing that with my acceding, it was done. The wheels of destiny were now in motion.

Time passed, and that encounter with Self in a place outside of time became a shimmering point in memory, its crystalline clarity retained but rarely recalled. It felt momentous, but remained inexplicable.

It would be many years before I would recall it again with the realization that it marked the beginning of a long life passage that would alter me for the better, but would bring anguish and despair before life eased again.

A Faltering

1996

FOR NO APPARENT REASON, I noticed fogginess in my thinking. It seemed as if I now had to punch through a cloudy gray curtain to see a completed thought concealed behind it. This slowing, plus lapses in my otherwise photographic memory, tightened my cognitive response to an unpleasant margin.

I was used to reasoning and planning what I would say far faster than the speed of my words. My mind dashed ahead, a little bored with the actual movement of my lips as they formed the words. I'd try on three or four ways to say something before the words spilled out at a normal pace. My mind could spin circles around the pace of speech for, per Mensa testing, my IQ was quite high.

Now the words passed from my lips at a pace equal to before, with the margin between thought and its utterance precipitously narrowed. I hoped that this wasn't apparent to others, for it could threaten my professional standing and then all the comforting accoutrements that accompanied this.

Other things were happening, too. *Why did my gums now bleed at the slightest provocation, and why were the whites of my eyes shot with magenta from the moment I arose from bed in the morning? Why was my face in a continuous blush?* Even my monthly cycle was off in a startling way, causing bleeding for up to thirty days at a time, stopping for just four or five days before beginning again.

I have no time for this, I thought. Aggravated by the inconvenience, I sporadically booked appointments with different specialists. This resulted in being I had gingivitis and dry eyes, plus a suggestion it was time to consider a hysterectomy, as "these things happen around forty."

But there were still planes to catch, meetings to conduct, proposals and technical documents to write, lectures to give, and speeches to deliver in corporate theaters and university halls scattered throughout the U.S.

I became distanced from Jonathan. Bereft of conversation while we sat before the TV eating take-out, I often went straight to bed after dinner. I was, by then, too tired to think clearly about what to do about these odd physical and mental problems. I was barely getting by. *Why was I so fatigued?*

Jonathan and I were in détente, the situation thus managed and controlled by default. Entertained by the TV, he spent his evenings alone as I slept.

More Information

Later in 1996

SEVERAL MONTHS PASSED before I saw my G.P. I'd gone to specialists for some of my mysterious complaints, although none had been resolved. The G.P. visit was an annual requirement of my employer. Why not bring up all of my odd complaints since I had to be there, anyway?

He had blood drawn, and later made an evening call to explain: Several of my blood cell lines were high, and I needed to see a hematologist ASAP.

Bargaining with him: "I have a cold. I'm run down, that's all. I sat next to a woman with a vicious cough on that last flight to Oakland!"

"No, that's not it. All of your counts, not just the white cells, are way off."

The next day, I met with a hematologist by the hospital in a nearby town. We met at his offices overlooking the sea, on a lovely summer afternoon. The sun beamed shafts of light through the windows as he said, "I believe that you have either a slow leakage of blood from a brain lesion or you have Polycythemia Vera."

After a moment to absorb this, I said "Really. . . can you spell that last thing? And what now?"

Explaining little, he insisted upon a brain scan and a bone marrow biopsy without delay. I had always been a healthy woman until this recent spiral downwards, and couldn't imagine ever being seriously sick.

In a daze, I first called Jonathan to let him know that I could not drive myself home after the procedures, and that I would need his help to retrieve both my car and me in about three hours. I cried uncharacteristically at the payphone outside of the clinic, as I explained both my need for help and what the doctor had said. Then, I walked to the hospital feeling very much alone.

In a few days, we knew that the brain scan was negative, but the marrow biopsy showed an overabundance of every type of blood cell. Releasing extra cells from bones into the bloodstream had created a traffic jam in my veins. Hence, my face and eyes were flush with blood. My menstrual periods went on endlessly as my body conducted a daily bloodletting to ease the venous pressure. It was why my gums bled so. Perhaps this was the dreadful reason that my thinking processes were diminishing.

Now the doctor could say I had either Polycythemia Vera (PV), or the stress related phenomenon of Secondary PV. He was unsure, because he didn't believe I was under stress although my variable counts, differing from one blood draw to the next, pointed to this.

In fact, he said, "I don't believe that women endure the stresses of men, so we'll continue observing for a while. I can't buy your theory that you are under stress."

You are trivializing what I do, I thought, but didn't say. It was common with men in the 1990s to be disrespectful to women in professional settings, although we were equals in all respects except gender, and I was used to proving myself rather than protesting their behavior.

Despite the personal offence, I knew how it worked. I thought: *If I am in danger, he will tell me, so I can put up with him for now.*

I went on to learn about PV, just like I had mastered the details in my technical field, which was for me to study on my own. I learned at the library that Secondary PV was a transient condition that, within the scope of things, was survivable for it would pass. If the PV was instead Primary, this was a permanent condition with a sketchy prognosis.

I decided I would get another opinion at a nearby medical college. Too bad I didn't follow through on this. Perhaps I could have stopped the high speed train of circumstances which led to the crash ahead of me. I continued with my prevaricating hematologist, and he continued to ruminate as he looked at the successive lab reports, thinking out loud like an absent-minded professor.

Through my research, I knew that PV was an "orphan" disease, called this because drug companies saw no profit in developing treatments for the mere handful of patients who had it. The sparse documentation that was available then pointed to its occurrence in Ashkenazi Jewish males, who usually died of either a stroke or a massive hemorrhage within a few years of onset. This information wasn't enough to conclude why I had it or what I should do, but if the doctor was unconcerned about my spiking counts, then I shouldn't be either, right?

These were my conscious thoughts, much like the movement on the surface of the waters I looked down upon from my home. What lay below in the depths was something else: My self-contained shock was escalating: Whatever this was, it was not a cold or flu or a cut or scrape. This was perhaps one of those life-impacting diseases that we always think only other people get.

I've never liked victimhood for this weakens a person. I reframed my situation to be, if true, a temporary setback. This was how I continued to control all the aspects of my life. If I was not under control beneath the surface, at least my outward appearance remained calm. I could work harder to compensate for these unforeseen complications. I told myself that all was still well in my world, as long as I didn't succumb to fright. This was the only enemy I could not control or manipulate. Without Librium, the sedative often prescribed at that time, I was powerless over panic, so I asked for a higher dosage and carried on.

Then, one January morning, perhaps seven or eight months after the diagnosis and treatment speculations had begun, I settled onto a bench in the kitchen nook, my head spun, and I collapsed to the tile floor.

Dying: to the Other Side and Back

January 21, 1997

I HAD NO CONTROL over the descent as my head led the way downwards to my right until I had slumped almost out of my seat, my body bowing down to the floor.

My startled husband reached over to prop me back up.

Once again I slumped over, head swinging low, just above the floor.

I saw the white tile and unfinished woods of my kitchen nook in duplicate. I saw double, and then triple, in a rolling shutter view, as I looked up to the beige and pink stripes of the drapes covering the sliders leading to the rose garden.

Jonathan carried me to the living room couch, away from the hard surfaces where I was floundering.

When I began projectile vomiting, he was sufficiently alarmed that he swept me up, still in my robe, and carried me to the car. We sped onto the El Camino Real, north on the two lane road toward the hospital, while I remained spinning in the passenger seat.

At the Emergency Room, I fought to retain speech and movement. I was losing, and soon could not reliably report or even gesture to my rescuers.

It was important to describe what I was experiencing! How could the E.R. doctor control what was happening unless I supplied information to him? I got a few words out. I even wrote a few phrases into the daily planner still beside my gurney, in case I soon could not communicate at all. *Seeing triple. Spinning.*

Then this became more than I could manage. I stopped moving and talking, and in the surreal moment when my night clothes were being cut away from me, I thought, *"Is this really happening?"* The male nurse, not wasting the seconds needed to take off my robe and gown in the normal way, then tossed a hospital gown onto me. He struggled as he started an I.V. in my left arm. With quick dispatch, my gurney was then trundled down a corridor, onto an elevator, and into a room that I realized had to be in intensive care.

My increasing lack of control catapulted me into uncharted territory, in which I could not communicate and could not defend myself. Next, the left side of my head felt as if it had blown a hole allowing my life to rush out. With the electric red splash of an explosion, my very essence was rocketing out of the ragged edges of a bright crimson hole, rimmed with blackness. The accompanying pain shot not only outward but inward, rebounding against all the fleshly boundaries of my body.

I heard raised voices, and saw increasing numbers of personnel in the room, as they jittered before me in double and then triple view. In green scrubs, or V-necked cotton tops with little balloons or ducks dancing in a row, with surgical caps tied at the back at their necks, they swarmed around me, and they were, it seemed, in a controlled panic.

Well, I thought, it was happening as quickly for them as it was for me! I could feel what was happening, but words wouldn't come. If they *knew* what was happening, they could only prop my slumping and paralyzed body within the hospital bed, and observe my countenance as they monitored my vitals.

Then, there was a pause in time, and as if in the space between the in-breath and the out-breath, I left my body.

Whoever or whatever I am, whether body or soul, I did not know in that moment. However defined, "I" moved toward a beautiful sunset-colored field of light in the upper left corner of the room and from there, watched what was going on down below.

What *was* that color? I'd never seen such beauty, and there was no name for it, for it was more subtle than anything I'd known with Earthly eyes. It was pink. No, it was like the honey soft blush of a ripening peach. It was like a cloud, and yet it was transparent. It was vibrating and glowing, illuminated from within. And it was so appealing that I wanted a closer look. In fact, I wanted to move right into it.

Beneath me, overwrought medical personnel surrounded my body registering their shock at how quickly my limbs had gone cold.

What was going on? What *was* this phenomenon I referred to as "I," after all? What I had thought of as limb, life, mind and soul had become separated. That which I thought of as "I" now existed apart from my body!

I had never separated from this body I had always thought of as "mine," and thus had concluded, until that moment, that "I" was a discrete feeling unit of flesh, albeit connected to others empathically. What a surprise to see through this experience that this was not true! How I wanted to tell the medical personnel, now working to save me! I was still alive and okay, and it was pointless to fret so much. *I'm still alive!*

Again I thought who *knew* that whatever discrete bit of intelligence and feeling I was, it could leave its symbiotic relationship with flesh? Why didn't this cause destruction, if "I" was separated from my bodily home? If only I could tell the others in the room with me I didn't feel attached to my body, and I no longer perceived feelings coming from it, and was observing their efforts but didn't want them to feel the fear and frustration that was emanating from them.

As a person experiences physical death, one realizes the preeminence of the mind and spirit. I knew in that moment that *bodies are temporary vehicles or tools.* I didn't just believe this in a theoretical sort of way. I *knew* it. I accepted what was happening, although I didn't understand it.

Without doubt, I knew I'd returned to an infinite pool of consciousness, keeping my individuality yet reunited with a larger whole.

I felt as if I was back home. Not my Earthly one, but my real home from which I came in order to live an Earthly life. I realized that as I *thought*, I was communicating with this larger whole or

Being that was home. It was responding to me. The Oneness I'd sensed before this, in childhood play and later in the light of my bedroom floor, had now proven itself. I was *in it.*

Both time and space disappeared in the instant I left my body, and I was, in this new state, overcome with joy at the realization that I, as an individual consciousness, could watch what was going on below, separate and yet also united with this infinite Presence. I'd made the transition from shock to delight!

It became apparent immediately that my life was an unfolding story in which I had recorded every second in my personal memory, but it was also recorded somewhere else beyond me. My memories were not only mine, but part of a collective consciousness that had recollections beyond what I was capable of, with what still seemed to be my human brain.

I knew that in the living of my life, I had calculated every move, assessed every variable, and then chosen my route based on logic and reason, although clearly not always so well!

Now the pause button had been hit, and I began a review, watching as if this were a video about to play from the beginning, my very beginning as Emily.

Enveloped in a vibrating field of sound, color and intense love, I realized that we would look back over my life. I say "we," for I now knew that I was not alone, and that I never had been. I had only *thought* I was alone as Emily Jean Entwistle. Now I knew that I had forgotten where I had come from, and that the curtain of my own Earthly consciousness had blocked my view of eternity. I realized that my life as Emily had been nothing more than a brief, almost instantaneous, interlude away from ALL THAT WAS, IS, AND ALWAYS WILL BE.

In this gentle and loving energy field, which held me as if inside a cocoon, yet stretched outwards from this central point that was me, we viewed prior actions and events from my short appearance in a body. Touching upon the events and feelings from childhood up to that moment, surprisingly, things that had seemed important in the living of it now seemed unworthy of mention. Simultaneous to this, it felt as though the confusing things in life fell into perspective, and all that had made me wonder now made sense.

The things I experienced before this moment were for a reason, and I no longer had an attachment to them, no longer felt either their satisfaction or sting. My life on Earth had been a little interlude in time, and here I was in eternity, and it was so PEACEFUL. And so full of LOVE. A love that said, "Everything is okay, everything has always been okay, and you are a wonderful creation." Everything that had transpired before my return home I now felt was perfect, despite what I'd thought during the living of it.

I saw that death is a continuation of life and that the other side is nothing to fear, nor is there shame in anything done during our separation from our true home. So much seemed trivial and unworthy of worry before this indescribable power that lovingly held me. All that was important, from this new perspective I seemed to be sharing with the limitless Beingness, were moments of love and respect and compassion toward myself and others.

I was clear about this sense of *We* rather than *me*. Yes, it was WE, with an exclamation point, for my boundaries without skin were ill defined and my sensations overlapped in every direction with those not generated by me. And what we glimpsed into, this video display of my life, seemed like just a flash from my entering my body before my birth, to my exiting of it now.

We focused on interactions and relationships, not the milestone events I would have ticked off, if still in a body. Just as it had been when in my empathic state as Emily, so it was during this review. It was the feelings, the nuance of energy exchanges with others, which mattered. What was the intention I held when interacting with them? How did my action affect them? *This is all that matters,* so my heart now said.

We focused only on perceptions and feelings. *Gosh, not that latest work project that I now was in no position to complete?* How silly I felt as soon as I thought this. How ignorant I had been, with my limited awareness as Emily.

Events and people that had not seemed significant before now were highlighted, to show how my internal changes always rippled out, provoking changes in those people and the ultimate outcomes of events.

Let me explain just one of these ripple effects we examined: Once there was a time when I was waiting at a bus stop in downtown L.A., at the end of a work day early in my career. My workday ended at 5 PM, and it was already dark, for it was winter time. My wedding ring's crest of diamonds was turned to the inside of my palm, so that only the narrow silver band was visible as I waited on the busy sidewalk.

A drunkard staggered toward me, and then sat down with his back leaning against the granite façade of the building behind us, and he asked, "Have any money?"

He was unshaven, dirty, and covered in clothes which were brownish gray with grime. His remaining stringy hair fell in a mess from his balding pate. Teeth missing, he grinned up at me, "You look like you could help me if you wanted to," he said.

"I could help you, but why don't you help yourself? Why are you living like this?" I answered, causing myself to wince at my own frankness.

His grin turned to a grimace, as he said, "I'm living like I want. What do you know? I don't need your advice."

I gave him a $20 bill, which at that time was real money. I had to agree, *who am I to judge?* Regardless of why, he needed help, and after I gave it, he arose and walked down the street.

He disappeared into the evening crowd of workers leaving the city. My bus arrived, and I too, left the city for home.

What I next saw in this video of my life, was what happened in the drunkard's life. Walking away with my gift, the man went to a convenience store and bought food, not alcohol, as I'd imagined he would. Later, speaking with bravado to street people about the young woman who challenged him, he brandished the results of my gift, and then shared food as they talked. He had not examined his behavior toward himself or others for quite some time, and had his reasons as do we all, but he thought about becoming more present to his true nature, and to want to be more. Growth came in fits and starts, and his new actions caused ripple effects in the thoughts and feelings of people surrounding him, as they moved into and then out of his life in the weeks and months that followed.

And so was I shown, in many more snippets from the trail of my existence through life as Emily, how I had affected others, and how they affected others, still. I saw the ripple effect of good turning to more good, when placed into this energy field we call life, that only appears to be tangible, impervious, and solid.

As the review proceeded, began, ended, I wasn't sure, for I was outside of time and space, and all was simultaneous rather than linear, I also thought, *"Wow! I never expected to leave this life so early!"*

How did I end up here at age forty-three when I had not planned it or foreseen it or manipulated this outcome in any way? How could I have overlooked the possibility I would die before I'd completed a normal life span?

As I was thinking this, I realized that I was in fact in a dialogue with this infinite Source or Energy of Home. I was re-united with an energy field I'd known before. I thought of looking for an anthropomorphized version of this field, like my Sunday School training had taught me, but it seemed pointless. The energy was alive, it was conscious, and it was omniscient. It was ALL THAT IS.

I marveled as it responded to me without judgment. I could disappoint myself but I could not disappoint It. It loved me. *It was love.*

The nature of It was unlike anything I had expected, for It was not an entity outside of myself, but part of the fabric of who I was, only It extended into infinity, so it seemed as I looked for Its boundaries. Was there anything I could experience that It was not? It became apparent, as I tested in my mind, that this vibrating field was an energetic form of love that knew all, sensed all, and had the spaciousness of limitless tolerance. All moved within it, and yet all remained the same. It was a paradox of motion within a field that was eternally motionless.

Was there a negative or a positive here? No, all movement was positive in Its perception! There were gradations of perfection, not rights and wrongs. There were only the slightest of moves necessary to see that what I'd interpreted as negative was positive. It depended upon the height from which one judged it from.

27

It did not feel goal oriented here, but it was not nothingness or pointlessness. Nor was I. We simply *were,* and I had existed well before playing in my blink-of-an-eye interlude away from home as Emily! Without any need for explanation, I saw for myself: We define Ourself in relationship to one another, little me and Higher me, or Higher Self. We are in our natural state, our Home, or perhaps home base, when together here on the other side.

I learned quickly that as I thought, It also thought. We were communicating, with my thoughts intersecting Its thoughts, and patterns of our harmony were forming, similar to what I'd done on Earth while in the company of others. But it was happening simultaneously—my thoughts and Its thoughts were resonating like a chord rather than a ping pong of notes in a point and counterpoint. We merged into a synthesis of thoughts, in a new yet old sensation of harmony now out of the Tick-Tock of time.

I asked, "Why did I leave Earth so soon?"

The answer, arriving simultaneously with my question, was "Why not? It makes no difference. You are eternal. Don't you see that life doesn't cease when you leave behind that broken body? You will have other chances to be in-body, if you wish."

Convinced by this logic, I was seduced by the entrancing pull toward joy which then pervaded and suffused me in the light.

Now I was merged into a vastness of ALL, and free to reacquaint myself with It, for I knew I was safely Home again. The love both embraced me and penetrated me. I was being welcomed back, and who could refuse this? Life in a body had its moments of beauty but was tainted by fright and pain, too, and perhaps I'd experienced enough for a lifetime, right?

I shifted toward acceptance. *That's how it's turned out. Surprise! My Earthly experience is over. I should get ready to go. Look forward, not behind.*

I'd noticed before this, that there was a wispy pathway to my right. It now shone more intensely, and seemed to entice me toward its starting point. A minor shift in attitude, and I would be on my way, drawn along in the lure of its pull. It felt like I needed to take a few steps toward it, and it felt like my former body used to when I was in motion, even though I could look back and see my physical body below me in the hospital bed with people gathered all around it, now quiet in the midst of the heart-sinking defeat of my unexpected death.

As if all the stops were pulled on a great cathedral organ, an overwhelming crescendo of vibration, a beyond-Earthly movement of love and peace and joy and rightness, swept me further into this decision to let the path move me, like boarding a rolling conveyor belt that would transport me away from further views of Earthly life. I was riding the crest of a wave on an ocean of joy and love that words cannot convey as I moved further into the energy field and toward the glimmering wisp of the light trail before me. It seemed that a movement away from my arrival point was required of me now, and I felt more than saw this as it was occurring.

But before I went deeper into the welcoming draw of this, I looked down to Earth again and fatefully thought, "What will happen to my husband?"

That instant I snapped back into my body.

Pain extended beyond my head throughout my entirety. In agony, I was paralyzed and unable to speak. My head was still packed on either side with pillows so I wouldn't slip top first, drooping over one side, out of the hospital bed.

"Welcome back. Our heads are very heavy, you know," said the nurse who remained, as she tried to mask her surprise.

My muscles, even those in my throat, were inaccessible to me, so a reply was impossible. *How did that work, again? What was the trick to getting them to respond when I wish them to?*

The next five days, I do not recall eating or moving. I regretted that I was sedated to the point where I could do little but sleep. I wanted to communicate with the personnel attending me, about what had happened and what could be done about the state I was in. Most of all, I wanted to say *don't numb these amazing sensations and insights with your drugs.*

You see, I was traveling in my etheric body here and there throughout the hospital, and had no way to tell them this.

The first experience of this was when I was still on the other side and noticed the man in the ICU room next to mine. The wall between our rooms seemed somehow transparent, and I could see him, all alone, and feel or hear his thoughts. He was anxious about dying without anyone noticing.

Once back from the other side, I slipped away from my physical body to join him energetically at his bedside. I told him he would not die alone. I would remain with him. The non-physical part of me communicated to the non-physical part of him,

"It will be okay. You'll see! You are not dying — you are only slipping away from your body and returning to your true self. I'll stay with you until it happens."

How lovely it was to experience the peace he felt, as he soon floated away from his damaged body.

I was left with an abiding desire to help others like him in their transitions. I wanted no one to be alone at that moment unless they chose to be.

I continued to practice this during my hospital stay and was to continue this for many years after, although I didn't know it then. What gratitude I have to this first man, who moved my heart to help him during his final moments in a body!

As for my own physical status, each day a phlebotomist would come to my bedside to remove a pint of blood from my body. The plan was evidently to thin my blood through the daily removal of heavy cell-laden plasma, diluting it with an influx of saline from a transparent bag suspended above me.

My blood vessels were impossible to prick, collapsing when hit with the needle, and beneath the skin they oozed when nicked. The soft inner sides of each arm had overlays of black, brown and yellow hematomas, and yet my blood would not come out of the veins, too thick to pass through the hollow needle into the technician's bag.

Excess blood was removed from my system and discarded as medical waste. Being defective, it was useless for others, and a danger to me.

These therapeutic phlebotomies, as they are called, were so difficult for the hospital staff, that they rotated through every member of the team until only one remained willing to work on my tiny veins, gritting her teeth as she'd try over and over again, in perhaps a half-a-dozen stabs, never to yield that precious whoosh of blood into the tubing that showed a direct connection to a vein.

With entrance achieved, there would be a little spurt, followed by stalled out and browning fluid within the flexible tubing never to make it to the vial, as each vein she tried collapsed from the shock of intrusion. Without taking the excess blood from my body I could not live, so I learned later. She saved my life through her persistent efforts.

What had happened to my body to have caused such a dramatic event as my departure from it, and then a return to precarious life? I did not then know from a medical perspective, but regardless I had died and gone to Heaven, and had returned to my abandoned and dead or dying body the instant I had a concern about the wellbeing of my husband.

Reflecting upon what I had experienced on the other side, I realized it was free will that caused my return to my body. When I did not agree with my movement toward Heaven, my desire to be present again in my body for the sake of another expressed itself instantly. Bam! Back in my messed-up body!

It was assumed, I imagine, that I could not comprehend a medical explanation at this point. No one tried. Also, it was unknown to me, at that time, whether Jonathan had received an explanation on my behalf.

Jonathan stood silently beside my hospital bed, now and then, as the days passed. He looked down at me, wordless, and always alone. He looked tired and still in his work attire when he checked on me.

During my stay in the ICU, I was moved by gurney to exam rooms now and then, and later learned that an MRI and a CT of the brain had been done. A neurologist arrived one day to look down upon me in the hospital bed with what seemed like kindness and sympathy. He said nothing to me.

Not being able to speak myself, and unable to leave the bed, there was nothing I could control except the inner world of my thoughts and emotions.

Days were passing, but it was difficult to know how many before I could move a bit and eke out a few words.

"My husband. . . is he coming?"

He eventually did, and then I was wheeled down to the car, to return home. Jonathan said nothing, and it took so much physical and mental effort for me to speak, that I was quiet, as well.

I could no longer balance myself upright, and with profound weakness, I could barely lift my arms or legs. I moved tentatively, using my hands to steady myself, into our home.

The Astronaut

1997

I'D HAD A DIRECT ENCOUNTER with the Eternal Beingness we've learned to call God, which I now think of as our Source, or the One. I returned to my body changed by this knowledge.

I was in a state of bliss, despite the physical pain and disability.

For the time being, I was no longer compelled to control anything.

I knew only that I had returned for Jonathan, despite the weaknesses in our relationship. The heavens had registered my concern for him as a signal to leave my true home soon after arriving, returning me to my body and this earthly existence.

I also knew that this thing we have called God was the energy and intelligence of love, and that I embodied this unimpeded since my return.

Dying had reminded me of my origins and united me with my Source, outside of time and space, during the period when I was out of my body. Now in the physical again, I returned to bodily existence renewed by Its goodness.

> I was dying amidst the mirage oases of Earth. Now the joyous waves of Thy Spirit engulf me. May I drown in Thine Ocean and live! (from Whispers from Eternity by Paramahansa Yogananda)

This became my gleaming native state. Having carried Heaven back with me into this bodily existence, I could suddenly observe the unfolding of events in both my life and the lives of others around me, with an inner knowing that all was well. Outer conditions did not deceive me as they once had. I knew now, innately, that everything in our experience is temporary, and that we are in constant motion within a sea of goodness. I knew deep in my heart that all experiences, if laid out on a line from least helpful to most helpful, were in a continuum of increasing amplifications of goodness. There was no pure evil as I had formerly thought. Nothing is separate from the One. There are only the contrived appearances of separation, caused by ignorance of this Oneness, or willful departures from the goodness. Neither can last, for the positive energy will eventually overcome all else. In this gradation from conscious separation to conscious union, it was still the One expressing Itself as the many. I had come back to my life knowing that there was only a gradation of expression, from weaker to stronger vibrations of love, rocking through eternity.

I knew that love shined both in periods when I was in tune with it, and when I was not, and that all human beings are continuously bathed in this. The spectacularly simple truth was that everything had always been okay, was okay now, and would remain okay. Not just for me, but for everyone.

I knew now it was through our relationships with each other that we come to know ourselves. Through relationships, we define and refine ourselves. We then grow in our own unique way, developing into our finest expression, becoming ourselves in all of our fullness.

I understood that this beautiful process could only be conceived by a Being, or what I could better perceive to be a benevolent energy field that is much greater than anything imaginable. Glowing with satisfaction, it was clear to me how everything was in its perfect place and unfolding just as it should be.

All of what seemed truth to me now, had been unknown to me before my passage to the other side. Leaving, then coming back with this new understanding, I realized that this rare experience had taught me in a way that very few others will be taught while living an earthly life. Imagine how it feels to be blessed with the awareness of blissful loving eternity Itself. Without doubt, without prevarication, without reserve. *To know it.*

We are asked to take the truth of our creator on faith. Now, this was the one thing I *knew* to be true.

I realized, no, knew without doubt, that on the other side if there was no time and space it was only during these Earthly experiences that we feel pressure to move ourselves along to new goals and to a greater appreciation of all that is. Outside of time and space, it makes no difference how long it takes for someone to achieve a spiritual understanding or milestone. It is all good exactly as it is.

And so, this was my inner experience.

In the manifest, however, I faced the patient work yet to do in the silence of my physical and mental isolation, since I had returned to Earthly life. It was necessary to restore my functionality if I was to be useful.

I had returned to a broken brain and body. It was all I could do to focus with whatever presented itself from one day to the next. Each day would, I knew, bring a challenge, and each time I'd get a little better at meeting it. Or not. This was still to be seen. I was still afloat in Heaven, although in a body once again.

I would either heal, or learn to work within these constraints. There was no going backward. There was only the future to improve upon.

I wanted self sufficiency. I wanted purpose. I wanted to serve. I wanted to be eternally filled with the light I had experienced on the other side, and to be a channel for this to all others, including Jonathan. If I could not communicate and move, how could I do this? Yes, I was still traveling and communicating outside of my body, too, but as a practical matter, it was now time to figure out how to make my body work again and to travel in the manner in which those surrounding me know and do.

My continued wish was to be a witness and a companion to anyone who was dying. It can be difficult for normal humans to stand by in the face of death. Many cannot do it and withdraw when the dying need connection. I felt compelled to do what others cannot, for I knew the limits of pain, but also that the ALL THAT IS is eternal love masquerading as an infinite number of things less than this. Attuned to others, in their homes and in ambulances and in hospital beds, I could be with them in spirit, but I wanted to move and speak, too, so I could achieve this in a way that the suffering could feel and see with their Earthly eyes.

Having returned from the other side, I knew that being eternal is not conditional upon any prior beliefs held by us. Nor is it based on vows of loyalty to God or Jesus. It doesn't matter if vows have been taken, or not. We are loved, regardless of our own ability to love in return. The humans I had returned to interact with might have belief systems different from mine, but we could all share in this love.

I had returned to what IS, and will always BE. Not "just left," but also "returned to." For

> When you no look no longer upon others as their flesh, seeing souls in everyone, your spirit is refreshed. Those who see the body act as if seen from afar. See the soul within at rest and see things as they are. Standpoints of eternity endow you with this view. (from Bhagavad Gita The Song Divine translated by Carl E Woodham)

it is no different whether on the other side, or in a body. We are eternal creatures. There was no judgment of my behavior by anyone or anything, other than myself, during my life review, and receiving this love, I felt only love for this *graciousness* that knew me as I am, sincere but flawed, in my estimation. Why should I not extend this to others?

I knew that now that I was back on Earth, here in a body in this freeze frame play we call life, no outward appearance is what it seems. We *recover* from every insult that might occur during what we are thinking, merely thinking, is our one chance at life. I was clear on what I was, and what was next to do in this movement or progression of beingness. I was clear on the inside.

However, the stroke (although no one had explained yet that this was what had happened) had taken most of my hearing in one ear. It also took away my ability to walk unassisted by props or people. I'd lost left hemisphere functionality and was now right brain dominant. I had difficulty swallowing, and food might travel into my sinuses or into my lungs as readily as it would correctly move down my esophagus. I couldn't reliably move my arms and legs (*Would they respond at all? And if so, the way I want them to?*), and when I turned my head, I was overcome by vertigo. The normal cadence of my life slowed to the pace of a snail, and I felt bone tired.

But one challenge stood out from the crowded field of challenges: I was not speaking well at all.

Being right brain dominant, I thought only in images rather than words. In this sea of images, all objects seemed in relationship with one another, rather than standing alone. Finding the correct descriptor for each piece part of what seemed like a shining and perfect whole, was difficult.

If I chose a word and spoke it, was it the right one? Often, no. It might be just the opposite.

I jested with myself, *this was a case of right church but wrong pew.* In my mental filing system, and just imagine the vastness of that for any of us, I might find the correct category but then take a wrong turn within it. For example, in the category of colors, if I had at least been able to speak a word, such as "white," the mental image of what I meant to utter was white, but the word that came out was "black." I hadn't intended to say "black," but didn't even realize that I had done so.

My bodily and mental changes were profound, and it would take time to re-acclimate to Earth, I thought. I couldn't grasp my new condition, let alone deal with the communication barrier that affected my relationships. There were not words to describe what I had experienced on the other side, nor words for the state in which I now found myself. And even if I had the words, it was unlikely that they would convey correctly from my mind to my lips to your ears.

I was confident I was eternal, and that I was floating in a sea of love more real than anything I could engage with through physicality or speech. Yet, I had little ability to reach out beyond this internal world other than when out of my body, helping others.

Don't look back, look only forward! Like an astronaut encapsulated in her own atmosphere, seeking to communicate beyond this through the endless barrier of space, I attempted to translate the right-brained images of thoughts into words, which often slipped just beyond my mental grasp, and once captured, might pass from my lips as the opposite of what I intended. *What the heck. . .*

What could I do but soften my internal reaction when not understood? It was for me to soothe, to comfort, and help myself, within the isolation of this.

Then I discovered that writing worked better than talking. It allowed me to reach out and seize the image, or sub-set of the whole I felt viscerally, and in time I might remember the sound and appearance of the word if on paper. Writing it down, I would put my note aside. Returning later, I stood a chance of noticing errors.

Communiqués like this were for special moments, being so laboriously crafted. The rest of the time, I remained unexpressed save by gestures.

And so I moved when able, in silence, with fingers lightly touching walls and furniture. Without this sensory input, I wobbled to the ground. Doorways and narrow passageways were the worst. In this new terrain of space and time, I would slam into hard surfaces as a matter of course because of my faulty navigation system.

A week after my release from the hospital, I left the house for the first time. A nearby member of my women's Bible study helped me to her car and then into a gathering in the warmly decorated home of our host. I wobbled and floated, yet was somehow moving.

We did not begin our study until I answered their questions.

Yes, I'd been in the hospital. My voice was weak and words came s-l-o-w-l-y. What a challenge translating from my world of images! I floated in a non-linear collection of sensations and memories, struggling as they sat in silence. They encouraged me with their gentle eyes as I tried and failed.

I bared my arms and heard gasps. Blood red, black and yellow, fresh from the dozens of needle sticks and blown veins, my arms spoke for me.

Then, with a few disjointed words, I think I said I'd died, and that I remembered it and it was *everything*. It is all we need to know. A life is only a short play. It isn't real. The other side, which we return to after a brief interlude in bodies, offers blissful reunion.

The ladies held their thoughts because of their indoctrination in Christianity. I felt their approbation and concern. Even before this, I'd had an esoteric approach to the Bible whereas they had not. What I told them did not match their beliefs.

Yet, in their kindness, they started a food delivery rotation for Jonathan and me.

One asked, "Don't we have to accept Jesus as our Savior for this to happen? Are you sure it was Heaven you had entered?"

It was disturbing to my lady friends that Jesus had not greeted me. How could my story be true? One by one, they distanced themselves.

Now alone with Jonathan, it was he who was the first to point out that my perception of the space surrounding me was truly skewed, confirming what I was experiencing but didn't know how to interpret. Perhaps this was neurologically based, or perhaps it was my awareness of my physical "footprint" that had changed, because I continued to crash into walls when I thought they were well enough away from my body that this couldn't occur, and then I would reel with the emotional shock and the physical assault with each ricochet off of immovable doorframes or drywall. So I accepted I must continue to extend my arms to touch objects around me even if they didn't seem close.

No longer hearing much through my left ear, all sounds reached me from my right side, so I could no longer judge directions of sound. Was that crash to my right or left, or perhaps behind me? I could not tell.

And so, why I resumed driving about three months after the stroke is a mystery. Was it perhaps because no one stopped me?

One of my first drives was to my employer. The fellow principals in our start-up company were happy with my coming in now and then to chat, they said. If I could greet potential investors in the business, this was enough.

After a few visits like this, I felt embarrassed and submitted my resignation. I wanted neither sympathy nor honor for what I'd once been, for I was that person no more. I then closed my private consulting business, too.

I wrote a note to my neurologist describing continued vertigo, which I handed to him during our appointment. Then, I laboriously explained, "If I'm spinning too much, I pull over until it passes. The whole world spins and I feel like vomiting." (At least this is what I intended to say. Imagine this with the words all mixed up and likely not at all descriptive of what I saw in my mind as I said them.)

"Well, let's see why this happens," said the man who had once stood at my bedside in the ICU. "Why don't you breathe in and out when I tell you, and we'll find out? Now, breathe in."

No sooner had I taken an in-breath, than he told me to breathe out, and then quickly back in again. Over and over, I huffed in and out at his command. Soon, I was dizzy and spinning away from my perch on the exam table.

"Ah, just like I thought. . . you are over-reacting. There's nothing wrong other than hyperventilation. Calm down, will you?" he said as he chuckled and patted my shoulder.

I can now say, in hindsight, that this was both manipulative and cruel. I knew that I was not hyperventilating when I was driving. All I was doing was glancing over my shoulder before changing lanes. Rapid breathing can cause hyperventilation in anyone, but I knew that this was not the reason for my vertigo in the car. In fact, my breathing was observably shallow and slow since returning home from the hospital. I knew that it was the shifting of my head that brought on the spinning.

"Well, how about if I order physical therapy for your neck and shoulders, young lady, and you'll soon be fine." He said nothing about my need to write notes, due to my inability to talk. Nor did he comment upon my hearing loss.

"Why don't you take a walk down the hall for me now, young lady, and we'll see how you walk," he said. Rising, the little man glanced at me and I read his inner feelings. No question. He was trying to hide something!

Keeping hold of the exam table, then with fingertips brushing against the walls of the exam room, I passed through the door frame into the hallway.

I walked, swaying and shimmying from the left and then the right, as I held my hands out, and wondered why he didn't notice how this extra sensory input was necessary to me. I knew that if I did not try to compensate, inertia would pull me down and over, on the side of my latest footfall.

"Superb, dear. Lovely," he said, as he passed the orders for physical therapy and escorted me out.

My hospital records did not support him, however. Something much more profound than a shoulder ache had occurred in ICU! Because of this, I applied for temporary disability. Although a pittance compared to my former income, it would help.

My husband's and my financial obligations would soon exceed our ability to meet them. Our lives would now veer far from the upper middle-class norm, and there was no one we could turn to for help. We had no one but ourselves, for our parents were deceased, we had no siblings, and no children capable of helping.

And were we a team now, like before? I wasn't communicating clearly with my husband, for so many reasons. There was my speaking problem. Also, he didn't understand what had happened to me physically, not to mention all my other emotional and spiritual dimensions, and he was perplexed about why I was now different.

It alarmed me when I learned that Jonathan did not know that when I was in Intensive Care, I'd had a stroke. Several weeks after leaving the hospital my hematologist implied this. The neurologist did not, as I've related, but I felt he was hiding the truth from me. *This had to be a case of doctors protecting doctors,* I thought.

Jonathan didn't know the truth and expected life to go back to normal. He didn't know what had happened, or what I was dealing with now.

He didn't know I'd died and come back during a stroke, so how could he understand my near-death union with Oneness if I tried to explain this incredibly important thing to him?

I held this thought within myself and pondered the ways I might talk to him about it. It was important to tell him what it was like on the other side. Shouldn't everyone know that we are eternal? Shouldn't Jonathan, in particular, learn of this from my first hand report?

Solo Flight

Later in 1997

MONTHS AFTER THE STROKE, WE SAT at an outdoor café in Laguna Beach. The trees surrounding the outdoor patio seemed to hug toward our table in the soft ocean breeze as I ventured to say, "Jonathan, were you aware that I died for a while after you rushed me to the hospital?" (Bear in mind that what I thought I was saying was likely just a few words hopefully resembling this.)

He looked startled, and while staring into my eyes, shook his head, *no.*

My speech slowed by pauses as I searched for words, I next said, "Honey, I went to Heaven for a while. I saw people in the ICU trying to save me from death, but it didn't work and it upset them that my body went so cold. I traveled to the next room and later returned to the man in it to help him die. I was inside a pinkish-peach glow and not in my body any more. It was so loving and peaceful, and I heard the most amazing music. I even felt it vibrating in me. I knew that I was back home with God, and being here again is so hard because my body doesn't work."

He continued looking at me as he shifted in his chair, and I continued, "Honey, I snapped back into my life with you again when I said, 'But what about Jonathan?'"

He continued fidgeting.

Cautiously, I asked, "Did you ask the doctors what happened?"

"Well, no. I had to keep doing business, and I couldn't be at the hospital often, but I checked on you, you know."

"So you don't know why I was in the hospital?"

"No, I just picked you up when they told me to," saying this as if it was what any reasonable person would have done.

The feelings coming off of him said *stop talking about this,* and I did. Never having believed in God himself, how could his wife have been with God? He must have thought, "How crazy!" I imagined he thought my childhood had made me different, and now I'd flipped.

And so he ignored what had happened. He ignored not just my hospital stay. He ignored my ongoing illness. We didn't speak of it again for years, except on one more occasion.

It happened when we sat beside a small inland lake during a day trip. We were looking across the shallow water when I ventured to speak again. "Jonathan, do you understand that the blood cancer is what caused my stroke?"

"What are you talking about? The PV? Is that for real? And that's *cancer*?" He turned to me, irritated.

"Yes. That's why you are taking me for phlebotomies every month! Gosh, I thought you knew. . . I'll always need them, and I should have gotten a better doctor before the stroke. I don't think this had to happen! My blood counts should have been corrected, not just watched. I needed treatment, not just observation. The counts went too high, and that's what caused the stroke."

His discomfort was back with a vengeance, but I had to continue since I had now started this. "Jonathan, it could happen again. I might die, or worse, I could become a vegetable. The cancer could cause another stroke worse than the last one. I'm not sure I'm being treated properly, even now, to prevent another one."

I waited for his answer, feeling that this was a test of his love for me.

"Well, I don't care if you get another opinion," was all he said. After more quiet passed between us, he ended the conversation by saying, "And don't expect me to do anything about their causing a stroke. I think people are lawyer crazy these days, and I don't want to fight any doctor in court. My life is too short to do that. We're moving on."

With this exchange, things solidified in my mind. It truly was just me and God now. I felt otherwise alone on Earth. Although prior to the stroke I would have told you that I had only the trappings of success, I had in fact met my three basic needs. Security, some semblance of a loving family, and my freedom had been mine.

Now I had lost all three.

I was plopped back into the Earth plane, after a brief sojourn in Heaven, and had no Earthly help. It didn't seem like Jonathan would desert me, but he didn't want to defend me, and I was in no shape to defend myself anymore.

How interesting, I thought, in a quasi-detached way. Had I not just been to Heaven, I would have reacted with intense hurt. Yet because I remained within that field of infinite love still fresh from the other side, I trusted even though feeling somehow betrayed. How could this be? It was as if I existed simultaneously on two planes, one being Heaven which was perfect, and the other being Earth, which was not at all perfect.

This dichotomy was clear and intransigent. I had to remain courageous about my challenging Earthly life, yet I also knew I was eternal and that it the long run, these challenges meant little. Returning to the play of life, my part was a difficult one, yet I thought, *it's only a play. But heck, this life experience feels pretty real!*

Again, I was in a trapeze act without a net. Another blood clot caused by PV could kill me or make me brain-dead. I couldn't work, couldn't care for myself, and now I knew that my spouse would only go so far to help me.

How ironic! I had returned from the bliss of being home in eternity when I said, "But what about my husband?"

Why? I had no idea why I'd felt so motivated to help him. Then I realized my love for him was not contingent upon reciprocity. I didn't love him because he loved me first, but because love was a flow that couldn't be stopped from traveling in and through me. Who knows why, but it was so. I'd felt compelled to return in order to help him, but it certainly appeared that I was the one who needed help, not him.

I was stunned to realize that I had no access to the next lines in the script in this play of life, and no understanding of my motivation as the "actress" for this scene or the next. What an ironic twist in this play, so I thought. And how utterly without the ability to control, it seemed. The control was now in Jonathan's court, not ours as a team, and not mine as an independent woman free to pick up and go if I felt uncared for.

In spite of this temporal fact, I knew without doubt that I had non-physical support all around and within me. My security would come to me through this. Through It: Source, Itself.

In fact, my soul remained afloat in the vastness of God, the primordial intelligence that had created me out of its own substance. Just me, alone in this altered state, unable to easily communicate with others outside this field of consciousness that I remained in. It was a world that, although it seemed as real as could be, I could not describe or share with Jonathan or anyone else.

Here I was in this unwieldy body, back in a world that seemed unreal. How would I survive? *Perhaps I won't. I'll soon be back on the other side,* I thought.

Travel for Answers

Summer, 1997
Heading to Scottsdale, AZ

'WOULD YOU HELP ME TRAVEL to Scottsdale, Jonathan? I want to get to Mayo." (Or at least I think it sounded like this. . . it is hard to know if the words came out as I'd intended them, and if the quizzical looks or aggravation might have been due to miscommunication on my part or poor reception of my words by the person hearing it.)

I wanted to get away from our home base, where all the doctors seemed inclined to defend one another. I knew I was still in present danger because my hematologist had given me chemotherapy pills that caused a plummet into pancytopenia. This is a condition in which one has far too few blood cells. This had piled fatigue on top of the fatigue caused by the stroke, and my mind and body barely worked at all. Yet, it had to if I was going to remain in my body.

Visibly nervous, the hematologist next stopped all treatment in order to let my blood counts rise after almost being wiped out. What a precarious position I seemed to be in.

To my request for help from Jonathan, his response was like a punch in my gut. I guess that my body was still reacting like a "normal" person's would. He said, "Well, I don't see how I could travel with you, because I can't leave the business. Guess you'll have to go by yourself."

Wow, I suppose I have to find a way, I thought. *Where to begin and how to navigate this?*

I would need medical records, surely. I asked my hematologist for them. With some agitation, he said, "Why? They are not relevant to your situation now. You don't need them."

I waited until a day when his office was open but he was away. *Surely his staff will help me,* I thought. Yet, the office manager had instructions not to copy the records without his permission. *Something to hide, perhaps?*

With only hospital records, I embarked on my journey alone. This time was unlike any trip I'd made for business. I pulled my suitcase through the airport staying close to the walls for balance. I moved quite slowly, with frequent stops to rest.

I still had enough mental function to board, and later disembark, alone. Feeling like a stranger in a strange land, I drifted to a rental counter in Phoenix Sky Harbor so that I might drive on to Scottsdale. Unfamiliar with the territory, and now dyslexic, too, I wasn't even able to read a map. Lost several times, I'm sure that it was prayer, in the form of crying out for help, which led me to the hotel and then the clinic.

After all this exertion, I could not communicate through the soupy fog of my mind. Not at all! I was like a blank slate, feeling lost and dependent upon others to see my need and meet it. I hadn't written anything in advance, either. I was new to writing my needs, and even less capable of speaking cogently and at a normal pace. But I had the hospital records, slides of my bone marrow, and scans of my brain, that this doctor's staff had passed to him upon my arrival at the clinic. To complete the picture, there were now results from a blood test taken just before the consult. As he viewed the lab results his voice cracked a bit as he said, "We need to take a trip down the hallway right now. Your counts are way too high."

At that moment, lightening struck the tree just outside our room, and we both shuddered. Monsoon season in the Phoenix Valley had begun, and torrents of rain poured down as the white flash illuminated us through our window overlooking the desert. I stood up, holding onto his desk, and he stabilized me as we went down the hall for a phlebotomy.

The next day I met with him again, and he offered to keep monitoring me remotely. On parting, he said, "Please understand that you definitely have PV, and have also had a major Central Nervous System (CNS) event. There will be complications and recovery time involved." "A stroke" would have been a plainer explanation than "a CNS event," something I later had to look up at the library to understand. But what my hometown hematologist had alluded to and then downplayed was true. What the hometown neurologist had obscured could not hide the truth, any longer. I'd had a brain stem stroke.

My Mayo expert said to think of my condition as similar to that of a lightning strike survivor. I had to acknowledge I was shot through with stabbing pain and tingling extremities. And it wasn't mere fatigue. It was muscle weakness and poor nerve signaling. And it was apparently a clot thrown during the stroke that had lodged in my auditory artery, which caused reduced hearing in my left ear. But not being able to speak well with my expert, there was so much that remained unclear to me.

There was so much different about my body since returning to it, and even if I'd written for days, it was unlikely I'd communicate this well. So during the first six months after returning to my body, I tried to quantify what else was off, hoping to do better at communication the next time I saw an expert. I began to capture details on a notepad as they floated through my awareness, trying to tease details out of the entire ball of wax that I was seeing all at once.

My eyes no longer shifted from a short to long range focus, as we take for granted. Sometimes I still saw double or triple, unable to blink these shimmering distortions away.

I wasn't digesting food right and wasn't breathing right. It seemed to take conscious effort for my autonomic functions weren't cutting it anymore.

My blood pressure vacillated from too high to too low, causing palpitations and then weakness that would drop me into my chair.

I had memory lapses. For example: I might walk to the mailbox. I'd first write a post-it note to myself about why I was leaving, then forget the note on the kitchen table, drift out of the house, close the door, and panic because I no longer knew why I was outside. And Jonathan would occasionally speak of an event we had experienced together that I could not recall.

I had little knowledge of what was being caused by the stroke versus the PV. I didn't realize it then, but I wasn't going to know until a decade later when my attention span and ability to research was somewhat restored, and I could either figure it out on my own, or better articulate my questions.

Because the local medical team didn't acknowledge or treat my stroke, and I had no access to the most important documents, I had no care besides physical therapy to reduce the hardness of my shoulder and neck muscles, coupled with orders from my Mayo Clinic doctor to moderate the blood cancer. It all baffled me, and what I couldn't overcome, I coped with. Jonathan asked no questions about my condition or treatment, so it was up to me and the benevolent direction I thought might come from the other side to sort out what to do.

For your sake, my compassionate but perhaps confused reader, here is what I'd actually come back to when I returned from the NDE, described from a medical perspective. . .

I had infarcts, in other words, clots, in multiple locations because of the slowing and congestion of my clogged blood flow throughout my body. The night before the stroke, I had lain only on my left side. This may have been why the impact seemed to rise up into my left ear, for the blood must have pooled there, but there must have been other clots elsewhere for I was rendered right brained and this implies broader damage to the left hemisphere.

Not only had my blood clumped into slow-moving sludge due to a shocking hematocrit of 64.5 (normal is a maximum of 45 or so), I also had radically diminished oxygen capacity within its red cells. According to medical experts, oxygen levels in the blood take a precipitous drop when one's hematocrit goes higher than 50, so I was well into the danger zone when the stroke occurred.

Based on an equally shocking platelet count of over 700,000 (normal is no more than 400,000), I was destined to clot or hemorrhage.

I'm betting on it being clots, because when looking at the scans myself, many years after the fact, I see no signs of a blood leak.

Whatever the cause, I was impacted in all three parts of the brainstem, and cranial nerves VIII through XI, and parts of the brain itself. Through my long-after-the-fact detective work, this has since become clearer.

Breathing rate, hearing and balance depend upon a working brain stem, and this had, in non-technical terms, blown up. Eye movements and visual processing need this part of the brain. It is the brain stem that controls motor movement. Parts of my cerebrum and cerebellum blew up, too. My long and short term memory crashed, and I lost the left brain functions like analytical thought, logic, language and speech.

With cranial nerve VIII blown out, I could no longer balance my head, or make proper sense of sound. Without a healthy cranial nerve IX, I couldn't swallow food without choking. Cranial nerve X, the infamous vagus nerve, controls the throat, larynx, esophagus, trachea, lungs, and heart. It affects digestion, relaxation, and controls consciousness itself. This nerve was affected perhaps more than any of the others.

The physical therapy I received afterwards must have been necessary due to damage of cranial nerve XI. This nerve affects the spinal cord, the trapezius, and other surrounding muscles. It is crucial to muscle movement of the shoulders and surrounding neck. This fried nerve was a likely contributor to the systemic neuropathy I also experienced until a few decades after the CNS event.

Most doctors believe that this type of stroke leads to death since the body has no control over vital functions. Yet, I had returned to such a body, after death had briefly occurred.

Now here's a part of the picture I couldn't really explain until I was capable of left brain functionality and could research adequately about fifteen years after the fact. Not understanding this, I felt embarrassment at the implication that maybe I was making things up or exaggerating my situation. But now I know the reason for the complete paralysis I had in the days after the stroke. This is what no one explained: Paralysis like I initially had occurs when there is a large stroke in the upper brain stem. This causes a break in the electrical connections between the brain and the body. Just as I'd experienced, it is possible to retain consciousness, but become completely paralyzed except for eye movement. This is called "locked-in syndrome." According to the medical literature, a stroke massive enough to cause this is fatal, as a rule. If it *doesn't* kill you, it's likely you'll remain locked-in forever! Yet, I returned to my body, and over time the syndrome diminished. I wasn't normal by any stretch, but I was no longer frozen into immobility.

Now, why did I have pain when a stroke is supposed to be painless? I suspect that what I was feeling was the starvation and death of my inner ear and its nerves when the artery feeding it was blocked.

And so, back to non-technical terms, I was beaten up and broken by the stroke! I was further broken by the uncontrolled blood cancer that remained. Emotionally I was damaged by being kept in the dark about what had happened, and not knowing what had occurred I was unable to take intelligent action to remedy my painful deficits. Denied stroke therapy and left to figure out what I could, I carried on with my intuition and my will to survive. And I was moving and breathing, at the level of my soul, with God.

In spite of my troubles with thinking, speaking, and moving, I felt life pulsing within me and sensed a hint of the purpose for my return. I didn't look back to what couldn't be changed. I kept my focus on what was ahead of me, and hoped for a better future.

The Inevitable Decision

Still later in 1997
Back in Southern California

HAVING RETURNED HOME from my first visit to the Mayo Clinic, I had a hard decision to make with Jonathan about our living conditions. I understood that I had a terminal blood cancer and there were medications I'd need to continue taking, but none would be curative. Treatment goals were limited to keeping me comfortable and safe from the more dangerous complications, while we awaited the end. Having blown my brain up, so to speak, I couldn't provide for myself now, and maybe not ever again.

Before the stroke, we'd planned on early retirement and had dreamed of travelling in an RV. Jonathan continued to carry on as if nothing had happened since those more carefree days, and was pressing me to do this now.

Why not travel for the enjoyment and freedom until the end of my days? I thought. It would cost much less than staying in place, and thus alleviate our financial dilemma.

My final days might come any time. PV progression is eight to ten years, and when I thought back on how long I'd been symptomatic, half of that time might well have passed. I could identify symptoms as far back as 1993 or 1994, and it was then 1997.

I believed what the medical literature and my doctors said about PV. *So why not retire and move into an RV now?*

It would also be easier than living in a house, so I thought, for the walls I depended on to keep upright would be close to one another. I'd be able to move my hands from countertop to table to chair since there were the smallest of gaps between each of them. And how difficult could it be to keep the 250 square feet of the little abode tidy?

And so I acceded to this concept, and soon we moved into a fifth wheel trailer. Parked on an ocean cliff, we could see down to where waves lapped in with a peaceful motion, each one never quite the same as the one preceding it.

The house sold quickly, and Jonathan's business sold after that. As soon as he recovered from surgery, our travels began. Yes, surgery! A few years prior, he'd started a business in which he worked outdoors, and was obligated to labor on in pain until the business sold. Jonathan had developed a hernia during his final months of work. After the procedure to fix this, I helped him through his convalescence. We then left, unencumbered, for parts unknown.

The Capsule

July 1998
All Across America

CONSIDERING OURSELVES RETIRED, we rolled away from California to Arizona, and on to New Mexico, Texas, and then far beyond, all the way to Florida. We clung first to the coastline of the Gulf of Mexico, then the shimmering ribbons of the Inter-Coastal Waterway, and lastly to the low rumble and roar of the Atlantic.

I directed Jonathan, the captain of our little home on wheels, in and out of camp spaces, and helped set up camp by pressing a few buttons and plugging in the cords and hoses that provided utilities to the RV.

I decided where we would go next, and how long we would stay. This involved map gazing, and a call from a pay phone to make reservations for our next stop. Preparing for these calls by creating careful notes, I seemed to communicate well enough to get by, and by studying the maps incessantly, I was now doing better with this aspect of my dyslexia.

I spoke little, other than at these moments on the phone. There were long silences between Jonathan and me. I thought, *at least it feels amicable.*

As we traveled, I had lab work and phlebotomies at local hospitals once a month. Back in Arizona, Mayo continued to enable my travels through remote monitoring. Because I'd have an abbreviated life with limited capabilities, I guess they knew that seeing the country and experiencing the people all along the way was good for my soul. I was touched by this, and remain grateful.

Along the way, I met so many people who were both curious and kind. I was self conscious about my limits, but the exuberance of travel made me bold. Communication still meant writing notes when talking seemed too laborious. Cut free from my moorings, in both the physical and the psychic sense, I found that I could adjust to anything.

Everything had changed from the life I'd once known. I was living in the moment, taking things as they were rather than how I might want them to be. I let go. I suppose you could say that I had little choice, but it was a welcome change from my pre-stroke life.

After perhaps ten months post-stroke, as we continued to travel, I had a very slow cadence that allowed words to proceed out of my mouth, but who knew what I might say? Sometimes I'd catch myself and re-state things. Mostly, my listener had to say, "What?" Or, "Is that what you meant?" I'd try again until I got it out right, or just smiled and let it go. It seemed that this worked okay during the very relaxed encounters I had in the RV parks with fellow travelers. This meant more faltering talk, and less note writing, in casual situations.

Before leaving California, I'd given away my library, most of my household goods, the inventory from a side-business, and much more. Life was pared down to only those essentials that could fit into the four hundred square feet of the trailer which is what we had to live in when the slide-outs were open and the fabric walls of the outdoor room beneath our awning were down. These were held in place by a sturdy rug that covered their long-tailed ends.

Before the near-death experience, I needed the material security and the marriage relationship I had with Jonathan. These defined me and protected me. Now, I knew that God was everything. I was able to strip down to almost nothing, materially, and if the relationship with Jonathan had no substance other than a forced togetherness, this seemed fine to me. Years later, I would lose this awareness, and cry out to God for help, but I had no glimpse into this future then and rested in His care.

I had saved only a few books, the primary one being my Bible. There was more than enough to stimulate my mind, my growth, and my daily observations of life in this one book. It was difficult to concentrate on any one thing and so circling back, again and again, to key passages, this led to increased understanding, and better retention abilities than I began with.

I also worked with cross stitch embroidery, thinking this would improve my eye-hand coordination plus exercise my mind. I focused on making first a perpetual wall calendar, and then a cover for my Bible.

I had studied the Bible on my own for several years before our travels began but when I dedicated myself now to only this book, it lit up with meaning, and I was led to multiple passages that, together, would provide a complete answer to any question I posed regarding the spiritual path. What a remarkable way for Source to speak to me!

Having been on the other side, the Bible no longer held mystery for me. It made total sense! There was an ethereal beauty to it that left me in a state of awe whenever I read it.

Asking, and expecting an answer, I would hold the closed book in my hands, and then easing my grip, it opened. Grateful to know where to look on that page, I'd get a partial response to my question, and then I'd know where to flip next, and next, until the answer was complete. Through this invisible guidance, I was taught more about surrender of control, about trust, about faith, about purpose. I took verses into contemplation, one after the other, until I had wrung deeper meanings from the passages, internalizing them.

As the scenery outside of the RV windows changed from desert to mountain to forest, from ocean to gulf to ocean again, this study of the Bible was a constant in my life. Occasionally, a radio broadcast augmented my studies. I was curious to know what the heartland of America listened to, having always lived close to major cities until then, and I discovered the syndicated Bible studies that are cast over the airwaves of the small towns of America.

Arriving in a new place, I would visit with the campers and folks near the park, and I was likely to be invited to the local church on Sunday. Jonathan would stay away from these events, so I tagged along with my new acquaintances, leaving him behind.

I had no intention of doing what came next. It simply occurred, over and over throughout the South. I received invitations to speak from the pulpit to the congregation! I spoke at many churches in my slow and laborious way. During the Bible studies that preceded the services, I found the passages my fingers would fly to could automatically answer the spiritual questions the congregants posed to me. Being silently guided to one passage after the next, what I read both comforted and guided them. We shared in our joy, and in seeking guidance and solace, our needs were met. It inspired the congregants, and although this made no sense to me, the pastor would often then ask that I speak to the congregation, choosing to forgo the sermon which I would extemporaneously deliver instead, in my labored but heartfelt way.

There was a great deal of love flowing to and from all of us, and it seemed natural at that point to speak to the crowds of what had happened to me, and how much love there was waiting for us on the other side, and how much love was available to us now if only we would seek it and dwell in it while still here in our bodies.

In one bitty little non-denominational church in southeastern Texas, the congregants were so kind that they lined up in two rows, arching their hands above me, for me to pass through as I left the podium. Many of them then touched my hand, or a shoulder, and gave me their blessings and thanks, agreeing to be reunited in love when we were on the other side once again. We all cried tears of joy and thanksgiving. Our hearts were so open to the Holy Spirit that it elevated us as a group to the refined vibrations of love I had experienced on the other side. Being in relationship with others of like persuasion always enhanced the state I was in since my return to the body.

In the company of fundamentalists, I, like many of them, would raise my hands like a child reaching for a hug, and then felt the love shower down. I knew that God was everything, and I rejoiced in unity with Him. I felt gratitude for the love flowing both to me and out from me, and praise bubbled up and out of me, praise for the blissful mystery of its unconditional grace.

Before the near-death experience, I had an awareness of something greater than myself, such as I now called Source or God, which I could use to improve my control of outcomes. It gave no bliss or sense of connection to something glorious or caring. I didn't surrender to it. I didn't have a love for it, and sensed no love from it. Now, I knew the truth and was immersed in it. There would come a time when I would no longer be immersed, and would sense the lack of it in a painful way, but I was not to face this for seven years. For now, I was in the beginning stages of what would be seven years of Samadhi. This is the state that Hindus define as a state of divine ecstasy as well as of superconscious perception. Christian saints have also described this experience, calling it the "mystical marriage."

Looking back at how I'd changed from executive to what seemed at times to be traveling evangelist, I had no idea why I had become ill with such a serious and life-impacting disease. Nor did I understand how my body could continue in spite of all the damage, especially the worst possible insult, which was my blown-up brain. But I knew that I was being sustained, one day at a time, and I was grateful to be useful to others now and then.

Each earthly moment was precious, since a fatal hemorrhage or stroke might occur at any moment due to incurable abnormalities in my blood. I lived in the NOW, from one moment to the next and the next, afraid of nothing for in eternity what is there to fear? My capabilities varied as those moments passed, and I remained steady in my resolve that I would do and feel whatever I could at that moment, until my moments in a body ended. A lot of my performance seemed dependent upon my energy level. Fatigue that usually set in before I even arose from bed in the morning robbed me of capabilities that would return for a brief while, but only if I spent most of my time at physical and mental rest.

Although I was in circumstances not of my own choosing, these adversities blessed me. I'd chosen to return to my body, although I didn't realize it would be a body that would remain broken in such profound ways. Yet, it was blissful to let the love flow through me, and it nonplussed me that it now presented me with opportunities to let the love shine onto others.

Although usually moving through pain, and with movement itself being sort of a gamble, I was remarkably still within this remnant of a body, here in the Earth plane. I accepted this, having believed, as I had long ago read in a little book called "The Practice of the Presence of God" by Brother Lawrence, that I should live in the moment and to say always "Thy will be done." Now it seemed quite natural to do this.

I assumed that it must be God's will to sustain me, but not to cure me, or He or It would have done so by now. I prayed The Lord's Prayer, and this soothed the distractions of pain and disability, as I repeatedly accepted God's will.

I prayed no other prayers for myself. Significantly, I didn't ask to be healed. But at least, I was praying to some form of Godhead, unlike my practice before the stroke. Even though I hadn't encountered a Being, but only Beingness, while on the other side, I still attempted praying to the Father, as Jesus had taught. But bear in mind that for me "father" is a charged word. It caused much ambivalence about the whole effort.

"Our Father, who art in Heaven, hallowed be Thy name. Thy kingdom come, Thy will be done on Earth as it is in Heaven." It was easy to surrender my will in this way only because I could place my focus upon being a channel for the love I knew as God. Certainly, I knew his Kingdom to be a Kingdom of love, and his will could be for nothing but loving outcomes. And I wanted everyone to experience Heaven so that they would not suffer so much on Earth.

I offered silent prayers for others wherever I met them. I prayed for those I did not know or meet, as well. I prayed at the sound of an ambulance siren, in particular; I prayed that the individual being rushed to help would know that they were not alone, and know that our Source loved them. I joined my heart to theirs and radiated love across to them. I had learned well that each day and every moment in relationship to others was precious, including those who until then had been strangers.

Because my physical and mental capabilities were in a state of flux, I might be capable of nothing more than sitting on my little couch in the trailer, while embroidering my calendar of days. The next day, I might be strong and balanced enough to venture out with Jonathan to the grocery store, followed by a little barbeque beside the trailer before bedtime. The next day, I might be capable of visiting with fellow campers for a few minutes. Every human being was immensely interesting to me, for I know how special we each are. Meeting others was delightful, but on the next day, I might need complete rest due to this.

I had no home, no roots. I had lost my health. My career was gone. My ability to provide for myself had vanished. I had no possessions, and no family other than Jonathan. It was questionable whether I had control of my mind, given that I was right-brained and nothing worked in linear fashion within it. All that was taking place in a given moment was like a fire hose of information blasting at me, and it was a neigh impossible challenge to focus on that which I chose to. I could communicate only with patience and hope that what I thought I said was indeed what I said. Yet, I felt one with the One, and this was everything to me. It was all that I needed, being thrown into a permanent state of NOW by a stroke and by the grace of our Source.

I will continue to live my simple life until it is no more, and BE THE LIGHT, I thought. Having lost many of my other capabilities, this was the one thing I could happily do.

I was now naturally inclined to do this. It was not me but what was moving through me. I was not the actor. I was only what was willingly acted upon, and this surrender was renewed with each consciously-taken breath.

I had received this message to BE THE LIGHT when I was a little girl. I was playing in my backyard, which was filled with heavy snow. Between two apple trees, where a hammock would swing in the summer, I packed the snow into a little tube and a half dome shelter, just large enough for a little girl like myself. I imagined that it was an igloo, and I completed the packing of snow inside, after crawling through the little passage way. Once within, I was surrounded by a white light which gleamed through the snowpack. It was not only the snow which now lit my world. I saw sparks of light all about me, felt immense love being directed at me, felt I could rest in the arms of these fairy-like sparklers of light now surrounding me, and I heard BE THE LIGHT. I felt comforted by the twinkling and darting lights, and I felt as if I were home and that I was loved and accepted and that I was to be protected by these benevolent emanations of light and love. I suppose that I had always had this protection, but now it was palpable to me, and I felt great joy, with a desire to remember and to do what they had said.

Do what the angelic protectors who have always been with you advised you to do. Be the light. This is enough. In fact, this is sufficient for all occasions and times, but we normally do not realize and practice this. We exist in an endless ocean of love. Permeated with this, I could not help but let its glorious excesses flow out from me like waves upon the waters, out to all else that is. For me, there was only a deep and settled joy from accepting and noting the rich and nuanced good in each moment, from sunrise to dusk. I was simply happy to *be*.

It made no matter to me if this was within or outside of a body. I knew that I was an eternal be-ing.

Broken But Still Useful

1999
On the Road

I CONTINUED TO WONDER, *why did I return for Jonathan when he seems not to need me, and he doesn't demonstrate any feelings for me anymore?*

The reasons were about to become apparent. I had certainly faltered mentally and physically. It wasn't apparent initially, but Jonathan was faltering too. He faced something he could not get through without my help, and I would gladly do whatever I could then, and so I found, always.

Prior to leaving California, Jonathan had struggled with the hernia that made working difficult. This was not his only physical challenge, however. Before leaving everything and beginning our RV life, we were entering a grocery market, he stumbled and said, "I have to sit down right now. I guess I have to tell you I can't feel my feet or legs. I'm all numb." He confessed, "This isn't the first time. It has been getting worse, to where I can't stand over ten minutes." He had quietly tolerated this physical betrayal, saying nothing about it until forced to do so. I imagined that this was how he was trained as a military officer to cope with whatever came up during a mission.

"Honey, I'll help you. We'll figure out what to do."

Later, when his doctor suspected that nerves in Jonathan's spine were being pinched, we went to a back surgeon. I took notes during the visit with this specialist. "Well, Jonathan, there are two ways we can approach this. I can do surgery, or we can try chiropractic and P.T. and see if you can avoid this step."

And Jonathan, without hesitation, replied, "Let's try everything but surgery," as I suspected he would. So Jonathan chose chiropractic, and after treatment he felt he'd be all right.

We left California thinking he could manage with short distances between stops to steady his legs, avoiding surgery, but this was not to be. While in Scottsdale to visit my doctor again, the numbness and weakness in Jonathan's legs had worsened, and we learned that if he didn't have surgery, he would lose the ability to walk.

After surgery, he would be encased a device called a turtle shell for three months, so in preparation we moved the RV north to avoid a convalescence in the Phoenix heat. Our plan was for him to recover in the cool forests of Northern Arizona, with our rig nestled up against the mountainside of a small college town. Leaving our rig there, we stayed in a Scottsdale motel with our three cats. Of course, I could not speak well, and could not move well, but I was getting by sufficiently to be of use to Jonathan. We checked him in to the hospital, and the surgery was soon underway.

After the eight hour surgery it was apparent to me that something was wrong. He was breathing oddly and seemed strangely giddy. I insisted that the doctor come to examine him. When he didn't, I resorted to writing notes which I passed to the nurses, as I thought I wasn't speaking quickly and clearly enough. Had I not been there to advocate for Jonathan, it is doubtful that he would have received help in time, for I seemed to be the only one aware that he was slipping into danger.

Jonathan had an embolism in his lung due to the long period under anesthesia, and proceeded to intensive care for eight long days, before the crisis passed and he was released. When we could finally leave the area, it was up to me to get us back to our rig. Our kitties, Piff, Purr, and Pasha, were in crates in the back seat. Jonathan, drugged heavily against the pain, was encased in his turtle shell next to me. Feeling like I'd sprung wings, I'd already climbed up into the truck bed to bungee our suitcases and supplies down behind us.

I had not driven since we'd left our California home, and had never driven the F350. It was an immense vehicle, with seating for six, and four back tires instead of the usual two, to support the weight of our trailer. There were multiple brake systems, of which I had only theoretical knowledge. This vehicle required steps to enter it, it was so massive. I had a drugged and debilitated husband in the passenger seat, and three mewling cats in the back, but I felt needed and responsible as I pointed the truck north.

Jonathan was oblivious to what was happening, thanks to a great deal of Percocet. I had a thin veneer of confidence, and this was enough to quell any fears he might have had. We climbed in altitude and the scenery changed from desert to forest, and I found my way back to the little RV park where we'd left our rig.

I had become a full time caregiver. I helped him shower and dress, then strapped him into the turtle shell that substituted for a spine while healing was occurring. His post-surgery body was much thinner, and the shell was far bigger than needed, but still serviceable.

He seemed changed, mentally and emotionally. Instead of occasional bouts of anger, he was now angry most of the time, always directed outwardly to me. He could not understand what I and others were saying to him, or what he was watching on TV. I assumed that this was because of the trauma he had been through, and that it would pass in time.

Before the first snow, we were once again on our way, ready or not, back on the road with Jonathan at the wheel. Jonathan needed close care and support for a year, as he gained strength and learned to cope with the spikes of pain that remained. Medications influenced both his mental focus and his frame of mind, so I imagined. He remained quarrelsome and confused, and the spinal fusion restricted his movement, so what he could no longer do, I did for us instead.

Like this, we traveled on again to Deming, then El Paso. After this, it was Austin, and then a big dip south for a long stay on the Rio Grande. Then on to the Bayou Country for months in Lafayette, a stay at Gretna Green, and then Mobile, Panama City Beach, and a long stay in Pensacola. Like always since my return to the body, I took joy in the beauty of nature and the changing geography as we moved along. The grand expressions of Source, here on Earth, continued to both astound and comfort me. It reminded me of the unspeakable beauty of the other side. But here in a body, I also took joy in meeting people along the way, and it was a privilege to be exposed to the panoply of approaches folks take, seemingly rooted in the land and the pervading culture. So many people! So many kindnesses! And I continued to speak in the churches along the way.

Responding to whatever was before me, I never questioned why this continued to happen, and did what was before me to do, as a grateful channel for a love more vast than I am capable of on my own.

One day, when we had moved on from Pensacola to Cape Canaveral, a blood test revealed that my platelets were clumping, and were gigantic. Automated equipment no longer worked on my strange blood, and lab techs had to count and categorize my cells, counting one-by-one, from a single drop under a microscope. They saw fragments, giant cells, immature cells sent out much too early into my bloodstream, and other strangeness.

Jonathan, thinking muddily for both of us, wished to bring an end to our travels. He didn't discuss it with me. I only came to understand that he made this decision on his own when we talked about it many years later. As he did not say otherwise, I continued to imagine that we would continue to travel full time, and that we were now just creating a home base for occasional breaks from the road.

Lost in Space Forever?

2000
On a barrier island in Florida

IT WAS ENJOYABLE LOOKING at small houses and condos on the Eastern shore of Florida where we had dropped the RV's jacks. It did not take long until we were living in a condominium building on the banks of a wide salt creek which flowed inland from the Pacific Ocean.

I still expected that we would take off soon, and anticipated seeing more of the Deep South, and then the Midwest. When this did not occur, I devoted time to researching "the disease," to frequent doctor visits and blood draws, and developing a list of out-of-state experts I'd eventually use for annual treks beyond Florida.

Settled in our condo, I again had reliable internet access. I thought with continued searching there, I might find a solution to the threat of blood clots I now faced because of my giant clumping platelets. The jacks, having dropped from the prow of the fifth wheel into the damp soil of the South, would not be rising soon, and the trailer waited, abandoned in a storage facility, for the infrequent visits that would keep its batteries watered.

I still remained in the cocoon of protective love that in fact covers us all, and I continued to shine that love out. I was researching the disease not out of fear, but my sense that I should be responsible about the body I again resided in. I knew that I was blessed beyond description as God's love flowed in and through me. Although no longer freely traveling the by-roads of America, I was still adrift in space, in all other ways. I had a little focus on my internet searches, but a lot of sensory overwhelm in the moment, with very little ability to articulate.

> I'm the taste of water and I light the moon and sun. I'm the sound of om and the strength in everyone. I'm the fragrance of the earth, the heat of fiery blazes. I'm the life of all that lives. (from Bhagavad Gita the Song Divine translated by Carl E Woodham)

My joy, and my appreciation of all creation, was heightened by observing nature. I would often sit by the windows of my enclosed balcony and see, down below in the brackish waters, schools of dolphins, bodies part shadow and part light, wavering below my seventh floor condo. How sweet it was to see a female manatee nudging her single offspring toward the tender shoots in the green waters by the shoreline, where the two would graze. Moving only a few feet per minute, this display of maternal affection and protection would nurture me perhaps more than their leafy food nurtured the benign and shapeless creatures below.

If Jonathan was curt or uncaring, the appropriate feelings never surfaced within me. I offered no objections because within my inner space there was only bliss. I floated in my own world, barely in my body. I looked only at the goodness all around me, and remained untouched as I cared for Jonathan's outward needs such as helping him to bathe and dress. Within this world, there was still nothing that needed controlling, to my mind. Outwardly passive, I remained in Samadhi and there was never a need for action to defend myself.

What I enjoyed taking action on was to call in rambunctious dolphins every morning! I found that by thinking of them and requesting their presence, they would come to frolic and mate just below me. And so, as the Sandhill Cranes promenaded along the waterfront, and the Great Blue Herons observed from the trees, I watched the dolphins.

> Rivers, streams, channels of abundant waters, and seas great and small, wondrous, diverse in colors, tastes and characters, Swarming with creatures great and small--- each one containing species without number. All laud and praise God with all their limbs, They constantly utter words and never deny their Ruler. Precious jewels and pearls glint in their depths: Hidden within them are the lights of their vessels. (From the Essential Rabbi Nachman translated by Avraham Greenbaum)

They carried my will to travel along with them, as they went about their daily trip inland and back. Their habit was to swim upstream for the day. Later, they would return to tell stories of their adventures. I listened to their wordless conversations while looking down upon them, once again, before their afternoon trek back to the sea.

A few more years passed, and I remained in this state of limited capabilities and inner bliss.

Circling Down to Earth

2002

OVER THE TWO YEARS SPENT in this high-rise condo by the water, I was slowly re-building the synapses within undamaged brain tissues.

In California, I'd been in an on-line support group for blood cancer. Having rejoined, I learned of doctors interested in PV, and what each phase of the disease looked and felt like. I learned that most patients were affected by brain fog and fatigue, but could find only one other who had survived a stroke like me. Others suffered treatment side effects, and with disease progression came a bloating of the torso while the limbs became spindly for lack of use. Most sufferers became apathetic and no longer fought to live, only hoping to stay comfortable and sane until the inevitable end. Those who proceeded with a bone marrow transplant, believing that this, the only route to wellness, would work, usually died a dreadful death of graft-versus-host disease instead.

In this grim environment, I made friendships, encouraging those who were going through frightening side effects to persist a little longer for the sake of children and spouses. And I wanted those who were lonely to know that if no one else could understand what they were feeling, I did. I still believed that I should focus with a single eye on being the light, and to do whatever the day required of me. It would take perhaps a few hours to write five or six sentences of guidance and comfort to someone, but I didn't let on to this. I hoped I was passing for normal in my postings.

No longer possessing the stamina and focus needed for the Type A personality style I once had, I couldn't multi-task. In fact, asked to focus on more than one thing at a time still feels like an electrical storm inside my brain. But I could recall my former mainstays of corporate life such as prioritization, organizing, researching, and discipline. Applying these skills again could make my life more comfortable and secure, yet these would come at a price. This strengthened my left brain again. As logic and reason returned my belief that PV would eventually kill me solidified, and now I viewed this as something to avoid at all cost.

I continued as Jonathan's caregiver, helping him shower and dress and looking out for him during his nights and days, but as I peeked through my own clouds, I started a fight against my own illness for my sake and his.

The nocebo effect ruled. The nocebo effect results from authoritatively given information that convinces you that you are ill, just the opposite of the placebo effect. I was thereby convinced that I could not avoid a dreadful end. I saw what Western Medicine told me to expect, playing out daily within the support group. I watched so many die I didn't question that this would in time happen to me, too, just as had been predicted by hematologists I'd seen.

But unlike the others, I still had a piece of Heaven in me, too. Maybe my soul was still outside of space and time, and the synapses of logic and linearity were still new and sparse. This dichotomy of thinking was inexplicable, really. Perhaps it was the battle between the thoughts of the mind, which are left brained, and the thoughts of the heart, which agree with the right brained state I was left in after the NDE. Or instead one could say that the little egoic self was beginning a clumsy tango with the Higher self that had reigned over all until then.

Being like this, I stood by my online friends. If an incarnation ended in a confused state of sadness, the empathic part of me cried along with my dying friend, but I also took the long view on this. It is not death we face, it is motion and change, and this is indeed the very essence of eternal life. I sensed what my friends felt, yet still being so close to the other side saw bliss in their future. It was no time for sermons from me, but instead for me to be a witness to their reality, just as it was. I would assure them it was surprisingly easy and pleasant when I let go of *my* body, but still I stood with them, in spirit, however it appeared to them to be.

I understood, just as I'd had the choice whether to return to my body or stay in Heaven, that we have free will. I also understood this life in the Earth plane to be an opportunity to use *my* will for good. There was very little else that I really needed to know, or to focus on, provided I thought through my heart, not my logical mind.

Just imagine all the simultaneous shifts within this Universe, sparkling with energy, as a light filled kaleidoscope, ever beautiful, in constant change. That is how I saw, in my heart of hearts, all of creation. Life is motion, life is change, and it is all beautiful, and we are gaining in wisdom and insight and discernment and finesse at creation as we collectively go on and on in glorious eternity.

Having acknowledged this underlying truth about life as I then knew it, what a surprise it was to now-and-then slap down to Earth in a more left-brained way regarding my own case. I thought that solutions could be found when I understood all the facts. Pushing myself to research the disease, I learned to analyze my own blood tests and biopsy results. Thanks to the explosion of information available on the internet, I came to believe that I understood as much as anyone about "my foe." Inclined to once again control and manipulate my own circumstances, I returned to the behavior that had proved to create a struggle, not peace, in my life prior to the stroke. I wasn't aware that I was returning to my flawed approach to life, at least not consciously. It seemed to me to be merely a return to normalcy.

I was ready to take charge after learning about a PV treatment considered to be at the experimental fringe, but showing promise. It was an injectable drug called interferon. The clumping giants had already caused two mini-strokes, also known as TIAs, and interferon had been found by clinicians to return platelets to normal size.

I began an online search for a doctor willing to prescribe it. Some patients who had tried before me didn't survive its harshness, succumbing to death perhaps because they were too far gone when they began treatment. Other patients experienced a slowdown in the disease progression, at the cost of killing their thyroid function. I saw no other way to control my own dangerous progression, and so I persisted until I found a hematologist in Gainesville willing to let me try.

It worked! The giant clumping platelets went back to normal, and the TIA risk diminished, but not without side effects: Lightheaded, I had unquenchable thirst and itched all over. Like running a flu that never ends, I was continually nauseated and feverish. I scratched my itchy skin until I bled. There were bald patches on my head, and the hair that remained became fine and sparse. And my thyroid was definitely failing. Now I needed an endocrinologist as well as a hematologist.

With fatigue beyond description, the effort of bathing and dressing was enough for most days, and I seldom ventured out of the house. I continued to read a few hours a day while resting on the balcony looking out at the water. In my mind's eye, I traveled Florida's coastlines, plus the inner scrub and tangle of brush between the Gulf and Pacific Ocean. I read not only the Bible now, but also about the wildlife and water fowl, and the early days when Europeans began moving into the land then inhabited by indigenous tribes of Indians. As my imagination soared, my awareness of the nausea and thirst diminished.

As I slowed down, Jonathan became restless. Now, finally, he was recovered from his back surgery, and no longer needed my help. Instead, he craved more activity. He was interested in joining a Senior Softball league, and knew of a place on the west coast of Florida where there were better softball fields and senior teams. I felt uplifted. Jonathan would have a better life if we moved there. Perhaps it would help to clear his thinking and cheer him up.

Crash Landing

2004
A new spot in Florida

WE MOVED TO THE GULF OF MEXICO side of Florida. The back of the home, looking east to the sunrise, overlooked an expansive pond, and the wide drainage canal that fed it was beside the north face of the house. Thus surrounded by pond and canal, I watched the hawks swoop down to catch fish, and the occasional alligator, cruising like a silent runner with nose and back breaking the water as the rest of its body remained submerged below.

Jonathan played first base on a large open field just a few blocks from our home. I continued to require constant rest, and did little else but read the Bible plus the holy books of many other religions, taking joy in the similarities I found within them all. Mystics of every religion and none at all, seemed to have knowledge of the place I'd been to, that place beyond time and space, that place of love and light and endless bliss.

After years of close attention to caring for Jonathan, his mood and mental clarity improved as I had hoped, and all was well. Long having missed female companionship, I made friends with a few ladies through a metaphysical book club, and once every week or two, I'd visit with them, followed by days of solitary rest. I was introduced to a few more ladies needing a witness and friend as their lives were ending, and was privileged to be with them as they faded and passed.

Now, although fatigued and capable of only a fraction of what I was able to do before becoming ill, my left-brain reasoning ability had returned with strength. My sense of linear and sequential motion, my logic and therefore my self-defense system, with the ability to control, was back again.

> The Kingdom of Heaven is also like a foolish woman carrying a load of flour on a long road; the sack splits and flour pours out, but she doesn't realize. Because she doesn't see what has happened, she isn't worried, but when she gets home her sack is empty. (from The Gospel of Thomas within The Gnostic Gospels translated by Alan Jacobs)

Both memories and words were intermittently blossoming, too. With this expanding reemergence into the experience of normal human life, my sense of the vastness of the One continued to recede. Perhaps, I could say, that it was put in perspective since I was rejoining soul to body, and inhabiting both it and this Earthly existence more deeply.

Unfortunately for me, I was working as closely with the events and people that populated my world, as I had prior to my NDE. I tried to manipulate my circumstances toward comfort and protection.

And although my mind was more functional, my body was less so. Still light headed and weak from interferon, I had poorly managed hypothyroidism that further exacerbated this. I was not to know until much later, but my thyroid condition extended to the pituitary, and this was why my treatment would remain incorrect and ineffective for over twenty years longer, until discovered. Although I now had some good moments, I was again confusing words after long silent pauses, and still inclined to crash into walls or collapse onto the pavement, and per the disease timeline, I was overdue for entering its end stage.

It was all that I could do to manage what happened next.

Further, Into Hell

2004-2007

WHILE JONATHAN AND I SAT OUTSIDE in the screen room one afternoon, watching the light dancing on the rippling water of the canal, he began to slip from his chair, giggling, saying that he didn't feel well.

"I'm gonna lie down," he said, as he stood and stepped, or rather staggered, toward the bedroom. Still giggling, quite uncharacteristically for this retired military man, he flopped onto the bed. He was rocking his head back and forth, and flushing pink, and then he started babbling in a nonsensical way and closed his eyes.

"Wait, don't drift off!" I said as I pulled on his arms to bring him upright again. When he angrily sat up, I coaxed him toward the garage and put him in the passenger seat of the car.

Under his protest, I drove him to an urgent care clinic. They advised me to rush further to the hospital. A heart attack was imminent. In fact, he had an angioplasty performed a few hours later to prevent this.

I waited outside the procedure room until the doctor emerged. He looked tired as he pulled back his surgical cap to reveal sweat beading on his forehead, saying, "It's a good thing you got him here. There was a 90% blockage in his aortic artery. I placed a stent, and he should recover nicely if he can follow directions."

The next day, Jonathan was told that he had to stop smoking his usual three packs of cigarettes a day, and that since he was pre-diabetic, he had to change his diet if he wanted to recover fully. He did not take this well.

Returning home, I focused on preparing appropriate meals for him. Breakfast, lunch, and dinner, this was quite an exertion, but I was needed and found the strength. Jonathan hated the diet and refused to comply with it. He also refused to stop smoking. He was much more contentious than he had ever been, arguing with the doctor and the nutritionist, and picking unendingly with me. He could no longer be appealed to with logic.

I stopped trying to help him change. He had projected his personal hell onto me, and I couldn't stand the heat. My own circumstances were worse still, despite the need for me to stay focused on caring for him. Incredibly, I had lost my ability to walk due to weakness, and used a cane for the short distances I limited myself to. Pain increased to a constant roar that made it difficult to think. My muscles, my bones, my nerves, everything hurt. I could find no relief no matter what I did, which did not include taking pain medications, for I feared overloading a liver already overburdened by interferon.

The blind faith I once held that my doctors knew what was best for me was over. Since I had studied all the aspects of my physical adversary, and felt I often knew as much or even more than they did, I now insisted that my doctors be a part of *my* team. I stated my position: Guide me to the best information and I'll decide. I added and deleted medical team members, based on who was the most educated, the most open, and the most supportive of the positions I already knew, based on my research, were correct for me. I had to double and triple check my reasoning as I went through this process, for I knew I wasn't completely linear and focused, and fatigue made it so very difficult to think.

Throughout all of the efforts to make good decisions, I remained aware of the stakes. I watched for signs of the move toward the final phase of the disease. I thought that perhaps the daily drumbeat of injections that made me sick, would not make me sick unto death, but would perhaps delay progression. The disease, called Myelofibrosis (MF) at its final stage, is unmerciful. Because one no longer makes blood in the volume needed for survival, it saps all remaining energy. The spleen bloats with immature and broken cells, with organ removal as the only treatment. The liver swells, too, but one must live with this. Then the blood lines irrevocably craze and lead to death.

Inevitably, the news of conversion came in a phone call from an expert I had seen. The brilliant doctor regretted to say, "The slides indicate that your pattern has changed now from PV to MF. If I look back on your prior two years' slides, I can see in hindsight that the shift to MF began back then, and wasn't fully clear until now. I would say you have had MF for quite some time now although we can't be precise. I'm sorry."

When I hung up the phone in the upstairs loft, I leaned over the balcony to look for Jonathan. Calling for him, seldom-seen tears began to flow. Seeing me, he said, "Don't be so dramatic. What's wrong?"

I slowly repeated what the doctor had said. Sobbing, I explained that the average life expectancy after MF onset was two years. Since the two years had already passed without the doctors being aware of it, I'd just received the stunning news that I was entering my final days.

Jonathan looked up at me, and as he walked away to the Florida Room, he said, "Suck it up."

With the sense of detachment I once had now gone, and my loved one withdrawing his support from me completely, I felt an onslaught of emotions rage through me, and I cried for days. No loving family, no security, no freedom. No comfort, no future here anymore. No hope of controlling the outcome. Now that the PV progression had culminated in MF, any gains made in stroke recovery were traded for a downturn in fatigue and pain from the cancer, which netted the same

> Be merciful to me, O Lord, for I am in distress; my eyes grow weak with sorrow, my soul and body with grief. My life is consumed by anguish and my years by groaning; my strength fails because of my affliction, and my bones grow weak. (Psalm 31:9-10)

result: I needed a cane for local navigation, and a wheelchair for longer excursions. My body now endured the after effects of the stroke, the symptoms of the blood cancer, the side effects of the interferon and more.

I was on over thirty drugs to treat the painful side effects of the cancer and the stroke, and the damage was plain in my digestive, endocrine, and respiratory systems. Red blood cells had become so sparse that on Sundays, I injected myself with yet another medication to increase them, in exchange for a boost that would last only until mid-week.

Jonathan now reacted with embarrassment, wishing to hide my condition from both friends and strangers. He was himself, in a period of good health, no longer suffering ill effects from his surgeries. He'd revived a bit since the placement of the stent in his heart and was ready to move on. I was his sick wife. He was not happy with being slowed down by me, and with caring for me when I needed his help.

I moved even more deeply into isolation, feeling as if there were glass walls enclosing me in a zone of pain through which I looked out, to normal life beyond them. These walls were, of course, invisible to others, and no one could imagine what was happening within them. I felt at that time that no one could have any sense of what it was like to live within these painful constraints, and what an effort it took to reach out from them.

Jonathan, tired of taking me to doctor visits, would grumble and say he would not do this any longer. When speaking with former high school friends, he prided himself on being a dutiful husband. He spoke of worrying about my wellbeing, and of doing all he could and more, to ensure my safety and comfort. Privately, he spoke differently to me. One day, he said he did not care if I died.

In fact, he was considering helping the process along. He said he would divorce me leaving me with no medical insurance that, with an orphan disease, would be a death sentence. I had such a rare disease that the basic medical care available to the indigent would be of no use in either palliative or protective ways. Only a few expensive experts in distant places knew what to do, and only with insurance would I have access to them.

Now incredibly far away from those times when I managed to control my own life and security, my husband was threatening me. How did this happen? I had been an independent woman, and now I depended on a person who had no sympathy for my situation, and wished me dead in order to ease his own emotional pain. We had been equal partners in all decisions. Now I had no say in anything. I was at his mercy, depending upon whether he had done well or poorly at his softball game that day. I was a total failure at controlling the outcomes of my life, so it appeared. Could I be loved, for certainly I could see little to love in myself if I considered myself as I used to based on my value as an executive and playmate in a material world?

> A man's spirit sustains him in sickness, but a crushed spirit who can bear? (Proverbs 18:14)

There were a few times of relative peace at the dinner table, when I would softly suggest, "If you cannot love me can you respect me as a fellow human being, and try not to hurt me?" I felt him cut himself off from me, and this stony rejection made me feel faint. Now and again over those sad years that followed, I would sometimes cry for hours while he sat, uncaring, in another room, hearing me but making no effort to comfort me. This pain sharpened to a fine point that reached to the heavens, when I cried out to God, "Take him or me, but I cannot bear this any longer as it is."

Jonathan wanted no more trips to see my specialists, and he wanted normalcy. If I could not pretend to be healthy and normal, he berated me. "I do not care or even believe that you are sick. I don't want you driving, and I won't drive you, if you say you've got an appointment. I don't care if you don't have your blood tested anymore, either. No more labs."

"But if I don't get it tested like always, I won't get the correct treatment to keep me from stroking out again."

"I don't care." And so it would go, in cycles of friction, followed by periods of silence. We went from war to détente and back to war again. I fought and begged for what was necessary to continue living, and Jonathan hated me for this.

I realized that to be resentful or angry or fearful was to cut myself off from the love that had flowed so beautifully to me for so many years, directly from our Source. I knew that to lash back at my tormenter would make my daily life more uncomfortable than to be quiet and submissive. I realized that I could pray for Jonathan's wellbeing, and trust that my needs would be met directly by my Creator, and that it was possible that this person who had once loved me but now did not, could still be used by the Creator to bring my good to me.

Then, I sought to control whatever I could around the edges of this massive and unwelcome burden that seemed to have no end. Somehow, Jonathan always relented, and drove me to my appointments with a hematologist in nearby Sarasota, but when I arranged for our annual trip to experts, he would not support me.

So my next bone marrow biopsy would have to be at my local doctor's office, and without anesthesia. It filled me with dread. This is a test best left to experts, which most local doctors are not. It begins with a wide-bore needle being forced through the bone of the iliac crest of the hip. Suction is then applied to draw soupy bone marrow from the bone's interior into a syringe.

As I rode beside Jonathan on the trip south to the appointment, we passed through watery expanses of river and swamp, lined with trees covered in kudzu. The vines, growing like weeds, tangled within the Great Oaks and other greenery, obscuring their shapes. They crept from tree to gutter, and into the freeway boundaries. I sought connection to Source in this tangled green scenery, punctuated by wide expanses of silvery blue water under the bridges we crossed. I tried to tune out the venomous words coming toward me from Jonathan. How he hated me! How he punished me because he felt trapped into helping me now.

We arrived at the doctor's office, and soon I was being prepped for the procedure. I found that I couldn't slip into the peace of Source. I searched my mind, crying out in silent desperation, for a God I could not find. I needed to be detached for there would be pain. When the procedure began, and searing heat shot from my hip throughout my body, I believe that I screamed. The doctor withdrew the needle before penetrating entirely through the bone and left the room.

The medical assistant asked me to take a sedative and relax. I didn't remember much else except foggy pain until being led to the car by Jonathan. He was aggravated now because the biopsy had been completed, and the wait for me to be released had, by his estimation, been long. Due to the heavy dose of sedatives I was extra wobbly as we exited.

He continued to berate me as we drove away. As he yelled hatefully at me about things I no longer remember, I began to vomit, and I flung my car door open at the intersection we'd paused in during a light change, and retched onto the concrete while holding onto the door's arm rest. Again, I silently cried to the heavens, asking for release. *Him or me, I don't care which. We cannot coexist.*

How can I explain this strange existence, as anything other than a state of bardo, in which I was not in Heaven nor was I on Earth? And my attempts to "manage" my life into a better state could do so very little.

At the same time, due to my magical experience on the other side during my death, I knew, at least intellectually, that I was always one with Spirit. A little part of me remained always in another world, feet not touching the ground. I knew that I was eternal and that once I returned to the other side, what I was now experiencing on Earth would be merely a little adjustment within the eternal motion of life. I clung to this knowledge that seemed less visceral and more heady than it used to be. Yet, my life was so painful, and my efforts to control it, to avoid the emotional and physical anguish, continued to fail. It seemed very real and had become intolerable.

I continued trusting in the principles of allopathic medicine for my care. I knew no better, and it seemed to be the only way to stay alive. I knew that it had measurable methods, provable through repeated testing. This was the empirical method, accessible only through those semi-Gods we look up to and call Doctor rather than by their given names, and it seemed sticking with them would be my only chance. I continued to research, speak to doctors, and inject myself with additional drugs as an alternative to the blood transfusions I'd otherwise need.

Jonathan's life was again in crisis, too. Yes, I knew that I should not be driving, but we had only each other, and when his heart again blocked, I rushed him to a second angioplasty procedure leaving him angrier than ever. Later, resuming softball, he was recruited by a team out of Atlanta, to play in cities up and down the Southeast coastline. He began to travel, leaving me at home alone for several days at a time. He seemed permanently changed after his many surgeries and heart catheterizations. It never felt safe when he was with me, and so his travels, although they felt like abandonment, were also a relief. Perhaps, I thought, he'd been damaged by anesthesia, now having had more than twenty hours of this in four years, but he seemed unaware of being different, and angry if I pointed this out. The issue was off limits to me.

Despite all he'd been through, he could function at a fairly high level physically once again, and was animated enough to give me a difficult time. I tried taking solace in this, re-casting this behavior as mere "feistiness."

How sad it was that after only a few years of near-normal physical action, Jonathan could no longer play softball. I learned the news when, calling me from a payphone, Jonathan said, "The coach is sending me home. I couldn't swing the bat. I couldn't feel it in my hands, and my arms wouldn't move right."

It was so disheartening to hear what the doctor later had to say. "Jonathan, I'm sorry but the condition we fixed in your lower back is in your neck now. If we do nothing, the prognosis is very poor. You'll lose feeling from the neck down if we don't operate."

Jonathan's celebrity within the senior softball world had spread; he had specialty bats that would sing with vibration as he hit the ball out of the park. He explained that he could not accept the hiatus that another surgery would require.

"Sir, your condition is so severe that it will eventually pinch off the spinal column and you will be paralyzed. We need to act quickly to prevent damage to the spinal cord." And so, we scheduled the surgery between Christmas and New Year's Eve. We had a month to prepare, and the ensuing periods of civility, although brief, helped me recall why I had come back from Heaven. Again, Jonathan would need me, and I would be there for him. Whatever it took, I was willing to do it. I did not think about rebuttal, or revenge, as one might imagine that I could have. I wanted only to help him.

And as for God, now seeming at times to be separate and distant, watching me dispassionately from above, I again prayed, "Thy will be done," believing that if God wished to help me, He would. I vowed to help Jonathan as long as I could move and breathe.

I was not well, of course. I'd come to dread nighttime visits to the bathroom, for I often passed out when there. Falling to the tile floor, I sometimes hit my head on the porcelain toilet and then the cold tile would comfort me as I returned to consciousness.

In my worst fall, which occurred just before we learned of Jonathan's new condition, I landed on my nose and cheek. Jonathan heard me when I fell with a crash to the tile floor. I had just missed hitting my face on the granite countertop. The damage could have been worse, I realized. He berated me for falling, and in the morning, drove me to the local ER. It appeared possible I had broken my cheekbone. Jonathan was, as usual, exuding anger. Looking as if someone had beaten me, and sensing the hostile energy emanating from my husband, they refused to administer treatment until they forced me to submit to a rape kit.

After this experience, I decided that if I must leave the bed during the night, I would crawl, not walk, from the bed to the bathroom, hoping with less of a shift in my blood pressure, this method would not trigger a faint. My doctor suspected that the vagus nerve was the cause, but could find no solution. The fainting would not stop, and became just one more thing to compensate for through extraordinary caution.

My life on the physical plane was in a downward spiral of bone pain, body-dragging fatigue, renewed speech difficulties, and two full pages of complications and prescription drugs on the Medical Summary I carried to doctor visits. I could no longer rise from a seated position without help. This was the state I was in, as I thought, *how much more?* I knew of no one who had ever been through so much, and felt that no one would want to hear about our plight, let alone believe it, for it was so challenging and sad. Was it possible that this was happening to other couples at this moment and possibly this happens all the time? It broke my heart considering this possibility.

I was by Jonathan's side through not only the first, but two additional spinal surgeries that left him unable to care for himself. After his cervical spine was rearranged in another nine hour surgery, additional surgeries were needed to excise an infection that had settled into it. It was eventually deemed unsafe to close the incision at all, and so the five inch long wound was left gaping open to the bone, covered with a suction device to draw the poisons out. If Jonathan's nurses didn't arrive when scheduled to maintain this, I often cleared away the infectious material myself.

My relationship with our Source was shifting in mysterious ways.

Angelic Intervention

Also during 2007
Around and about Florida

DURING THE FIRST SURGERY to fuse Jonathan's neck bones he began to pass away on the operating table, and twice again, while in recovery.

My story becomes a mysterious mix of darkness and light now. . . . After Jonathan stabilized, I went back to my hotel room to rest and reflect. I thought, *why does God allow such suffering?* And as I slipped deeper into stillness, I saw and felt duality disappearing. The answer came: There is no life, no death, only light. Only motion within that light. Would we ever reach for that light if we did not feel its opposite? The seeming tragedy was only this motion — why should we despair over what is temporary? Everything will be okay; everything *is* okay and unfolding as it should.

Knowing this, I moved through the shadow play of driving us to each of his distant medical center surgeries and then a frightful ten-day period in a local hospital when the infection overcame him. While there, he was given only pain medication. The hospitalist refused to examine the surgical site because "we didn't perform the surgery." Incredibly, I brought supplies daily and changed Jonathan's bandages because no one else would. It appeared that Jonathan would die because of lack of care even though in a hospital bed! I walked the halls of his ward, keening like a momma cat whose kitten is injured, demanding that the case manager take action. Victory came, after three days of tears. A bed was found in the hospital he'd had surgery at, and Jonathan would travel 150 miles by ambulance to get to it.

The case manager said, "The ambulance will leave in two hours. If you would like to follow your husband you will need to be back by then."

I rushed to the elevator, knowing that the drive, one way, was at least forty-five minutes. So very overwhelmed, I boarded the elevator and pressed the button to descend to the parking lot.

It was then that I noticed I was not alone. A woman with a clerical collar smiled at me and assessed my condition. She said simply, "What is happening?"

I blurted out how ill Jonathan was, and that I was not well either, and needed to get home and back in nearly impossible time if I was to be present when he was checked into the distant medical center.

"Dear, you are never alone. That's why you got onto this elevator. You needed to hear this now, and I am here to tell you. I'll be praying for you as you do what you must now. I'll be with you in spirit. We'll keep watching out for you," she said.

What did she mean when she said "We?"

The traffic seemed to move just ahead of my car as I sped home. My neighbor saw me arrive and ran over saying, "What do you need?" We packed my bag together, and again, no traffic impeded my trip back. I sat with Jonathan before the ambulance crew arrived, and assured him that all would be well now.

Upon arrival, Jonathan was taken directly into surgery. Many hours later when I left the recovery room, I walked with one hand on my cane and the other trailing the hospital wall, into the elevator to head down to the parking lot. The existing occupants fluttered and made a space for me. I had joined three men in the little space of that elevator and observed that each was dressed in black with a white clerical collar. They smiled at me, smiles that were genuine and strong and uplifting, and each wished me well. One said, "We never go through challenges alone."

This was certainly strange, I thought, to be having another elevator encounter with clergy offering conversation. But I felt uplifted by this and began to feel that indeed I was not alone.

It was dusk as I walked out to the hospital parking lot. There were streaks of pink remaining in the western sky, but it would soon be dark and I would have to check into a hotel, find takeout food, and hope to sleep before returning to the hospital for early morning rounds. There under the light by my car stood another man dressed in black. Did he have a clerical collar? I felt both giddy and startled by the confirmation. Yes, he was also a cleric, and he smiled at me as he stood under the pool of light.

"I seem to have forgotten where I parked my car. But how are you, my dear? It is difficult, but not impossible to get through trials when you know you are not alone. And you are not, child."

A tear escaping my overflowing eyes, I thanked him, and wished him well finding his car.

I was to see clerics bearing messages, wherever I went in the following days, and I never felt alone. I was buoyed up by the love that seemed to be beaming non-stop at me when I needed it most.

Jonathan had more dreadful close encounters with death than anyone can bear to read, or me to write, and I shall not describe this further to spare us all. While this occurred, I delayed a change in my own treatment. I had planned to switch to a new interferon formulation I believed would reduce my pain and fatigue. It would require very close work with a specialist to make the change, and this was time that I would not have for almost a year into Jonathan's latest crisis period. There would be suffering involved for me, but my purpose at that time was to alleviate Jonathan's suffering, not my own.

Poor Jonathan. What dreadful circumstances we now both endured. My heart opened knowing we had both done as well as we were able. We loved as best we knew how.

We were much too young for the retirement home that, in truth, we needed now, finding only one that would waive the minimum age requirement of sixty-five. Jonathan qualified but I didn't. I imagined that Jonathan would receive care this way, if I died first. But in the end, something stopped us from moving in. We agreed instead, we would have to find another way.

Although aware that I was the child of a loving creator, a part of a larger whole that was pure love, I had been trying once again to control the circumstances of my life and I had failed. Like before, this resulted in pain, isolation, and fear. My prayers were little more than screams from the pain, or resignation to my circumstances. I had tasted of success in life, but could not hold on to it for very long. Perhaps I was not equipped for life. I never "got the manual" and never figured it out. Maybe I was too damaged to do better. It is only now that I can say that I had little understanding of humility, and what the results of this could be. At that juncture, I was out of ideas and out of time, and was unacquainted with the deliberate gesture of humility.

My near death experience, and my unforgettable journey to the other side, had given me the inspiration to continue living in my body after returning to it. It had given me the grace to love, although not perfectly, even when I was not loved in return. Yet, I had reverted to my former ways: I again used reason and logic to control the outcomes in the daily circumstances of my life, standing alone against what I could not accept, although this never worked. I did not know what else to do, but was touched by the love that seemed directed toward me through the angelic clerics during my recent trials. It felt undeserved. It felt like what I was to come to know deeply as grace.

II

WORKING WITH
BELIEFS

The kingdom of Heaven is like a mustard seed that someone took and sowed in his field. It is the smallest of all the seeds, but when it has grown it is the greatest of shrubs, and becomes a tree, so that the birds of the air come and make nests in its branches.
Matthew 13:31-32

AFTER ALL HAD FAILED, I sought to know God above all else, through devout meditation, and then grace rushed in. It guided me until I understood how my beliefs result in my experiences. In knowing God, I also came to know myself and to change those qualities that had held me back.

When I no longer hoped but instead trusted, my experiences shifted from negative to positive in nature. I was taught to control my life at its generation point, or creation point, instead of controlling the after effects as I had before. I learned to work with causes, rather than my old way of working with the detritus of effects, and learned that this was what the esoteric teaching of the New Testament of the Bible is about. Through meditation, I learned that I had not been creating what I desired in life, but more of what I expected from both conscious and subconscious thought "ruts." After proving this to myself through experimentation, I reached what seemed to me to be a refined new experience of life. . . one in which goodness without could come from goodness within.

Changes occurred in sequence: First, my spiritual condition improved, then my bodily health improved, and lastly, my mental state healed. It did not come easily. When I tried and failed to remain positive, it became apparent that my unconscious thoughts were sabotaging my conscious efforts. Formed in the womb, amplified in childhood, and reinforced in adulthood, these beliefs had affected my mental state, my bodily health, and my spiritual condition all of my life.

Although I learned how to re-program my subconscious mind so healing could occur, all such change began with my direct connection to Source, or God. It was a gift of grace, and my efforts were restricted to using the tools presented to me by my inner guides so that I would not reject the healing that had already been given to me. When I was well on all levels, living a life of joy, it was then that I realized I had not been reaching to God so much as I had been pulled toward It. All that I'd received was grace, given in love.

The Mystic Path

Spring 2008

KNOWING THAT THE END WAS UPON ME, and that there was no more that could be done on Earth to save me, I turned to Heaven in a way that I never had before.

In the quiet of my home, I cried out to God.

If you are there, prove yourself! Make your presence known to me. Let me feel it and know it and understand why life is this way for me!

I know that you exist, so guide me now!

I want to have the joy of awareness of you here in my body, like I once did on the other side. All I have experienced since the seven years of bliss has been continued trying and failing. Life has become so hard and painful and so very sad.

I can't create lasting goodness on my own. I don't know how.

I am powerless and all I can think to do is turn my attention to you and nothing else. This is all that is left to try.

I wistfully recalled the bliss of union outside of a body. Since returning to my body, the bliss I carried back with me did nothing to help me heal. Although I had many years of joy and detachment, my body had further deteriorated and my spirit eventually had fainted with despair.

I want, more than I have ever wanted anything, the feeling that all is well, the feeling of wholeness and being Home, this time inside of my body here on Earth, not just the memory of what it was like when outside of it.

If I die again soon, I understand and accept this. But I ask with all of my yearning and focus now: May I feel the peace of reunion with You for at least one moment before it is time to leave this incarnation as Emily?

I cried to the heavens I so missed. I ached for this alone. It was my obsession.

What followed on the heels of this cry to God was the compunction to meditate like I never had before. I craved time in meditation. I yearned for the deep and the still, yet this remained elusive.

I began a regular practice of meditating for a half hour every day. Then half an hour, twice a day. Then one hour, twice a day. My mind wandering off in incessant chatter of this and that and nothing at all, and over and over, I pulled it back to receptivity. I spent the early days and weeks pursuing and failing.

I meditated on silence alone. I meditated on qualities of love, pity, joy, impurity, and serenity, as the Buddha had said to do. I meditated on surrendering myself hoping something other than me would be revealed. In time I would meditate upon the qualities of God, that Emmet Fox describes in his books, and meditated upon the qualities of Christ. I would even meditate upon both Eastern and Western qualities of Spirit. I focused in Paramahansa Yogananda's special way upon my breath.

> Be still before the Lord and wait patiently for him. (Psalm 37:7)
>
> I wait for you, O Lord; you will answer, O Lord my God. (Psalm 38:15)
>
> Within your temple, O God, we meditate on your unfailing love. (Psalm 48:9)

I surrendered all notions of what God was, according to others. I let go of the opinions of every religion I'd studied. I sought what I had experienced on the other side, and the blissful years which had followed it, before I had taken over the control of my life once again.

I contemplated the qualities of that life I'd lived in my seven years of Samadhi, those days when I acted and felt not from the level of my little self, but was directed by that larger and greater and beautiful energy of love that is "all that is." It had once engulfed me and flowed out to others because I lived simply, in truth. Or so it had felt at that time. What was truth? What I felt then or what I was feeling now, in my despair?

After dozens and dozens of hours of restless meditation had occurred, a singular instruction floated into my awareness: Listen. When the mind wanders, pull it back. It may wander quite a while before you realize that it has done so. That's okay. Do not be angry with yourself or with the process. Just return to your seed thought. Each moment of nothingness is a gift. The use of a seed thought (a mantra or phrase) or observing an action (like breath) was to focus my mind, disciplining it until I became open to the One's presence and guidance.

Try this yourself: Be receptive in the silence. Anticipate connection, or communion. Be patient. Wait as long as it takes. If it doesn't happen now, look forward to the next time, for it may happen then.

As I did so, I knew that this was the meditative practice of an adult, not the child that once began this so many years ago. I recalled how my practice began when about twelve or thirteen years old. This was much different. At that time, I learned the Salutation of the Sun asanas or yoga positions from a book found at a garage sale, and this daily practice, concluding with the candle flame and softened eyes, had evolved naturally into a meditative state. I had continued this practice off and on over the ensuing years into my adulthood.

I imagine that I learned as much as was possible from meditation back then. I didn't have the urgency of pain and possible demise to spur me to the next level. It was suffering that brought me to this point.

And so now, as I meditated first in the morning and then again after dinner, I waited for a direct encounter. I was slightly eager, deliberately open and inexplicably happy at the thought that the Presence might re-appear to me now, here in this failing body and in this failing life.

I looked forward to these periods in the silence, quieting myself first with a few easy Hatha Yoga positions and a bit of healing breath work called Pranayama. I'd remembered the peaceful strength of my youthful practice, and how the power to meditate was in concentrating the mind on the single objective of breath control. I rediscovered, like the yogis of old, that these physical practices bring an organic movement into the silence. And in that silence, I sought a direct connection with God.

My single focus of being one with the One remained with me as I went about my day. I continued to care for my husband's needs, and to medicate myself as the doctors instructed, believing without mental drift or doubt, that the powerful spiritual union I knew was possible was perhaps imminent. If the presence I'd experienced on the other side could be purely felt while in a body, then I would have it! It would disappoint me if any less than this occurred, but I let such thoughts of disappointment flit quickly through and then out of my mind.

My focus would not be upon failure. I would be as patient as necessary, yet I knew that my time was short. It *was* possible that this would not happen before my death. I accepted that this was not in my hands, although filled with unending hope that surely this one great thing would be achieved before my life ended.

I learned about guided meditation. Using headphones, I listened to audio tracks designed to create successful journeys toward God or one's own highest self. I wanted to deepen my focus, and when an inner voice directed me to seek this help, I found it. These meditation tracks were quite special, being infused with an underpinning of music holding brainwave technology that would integrate the right and left hemispheres of my brain. The creative, non-linear side of my mind, that side which was, I believe, an inlet off of the great sea of Source, was being connected to that logical, linear side of my mind, as I took the meditative journey.

Day after day, I resumed that journey, and was now in silent meditation for two hours a day, plus an hour of mid-day guided meditation upon the wellness, connection, peace and love we gain when connected to our Source.

Perhaps over time I had reprogrammed myself to see, like the first glimmer of sunrise after the darkness of night, that healing was possible. I cannot say for sure. This was not my goal, but a surprising side benefit of seeking spiritual connection like I'd had on the other side. This notion that healing was possible was a tiny seed, germinating under the ground of my consciousness that I was barely aware of.

If you would like to learn to meditate, or strengthen your existing practice, I hope that you will seek out books, teachers, and Source Itself, for teaching. You will be drawn to the tools most helpful to your own practice, if you only become quiet, talk to God about your situation, and ask for an influx of guidance. Synchronicity will take care of the rest.

Direct Encounter

Summer 2008

I SOUGHT NO NEW THEOLOGY. I also rejected all theologies I had learned.

I thought about all the "isms" I had experienced. . . for example, Presbyterianism, Catholicism, Buddhism, and so forth. I wanted no more "isms." I was not interested in "how" but "what" and "where." Surely there were no religious dictates, with priests or monks as its arbiters, to prevent me from re-connecting to our Source?

I was not taking anyone else's word for it, no matter how great the scholar or saint. I wanted to meet my Source face-to-face and learn directly from Him, Her or It.

Actually, I knew that at least in my experience, it was an "It" that I pursued, and I wanted reunion with It, since I had lost touch with such glorious immediacy of Presence, in the challenging years that had ensued after my fall from Samadhi, my seven years of bliss after the NDE. When I'd prayed up until then it was like a child, and there was a dissonance between my calling upon "the Father" and my personal experience of the Absolute. I cried out to my childhood "God" out of desperation and hope that there was a Being that heard me. I begged. I supplicated. I waited and felt perhaps I was not heard or my pleas were not important enough to

> But seek first his kingdom and his righteousness, and all these things will be given to you as well. (Matthew 6:33)

be responded to. I'd concluded that there was no Being to supplicate to --- there was only an amorphous energy field that I'd not even known had loving qualities until on the other side.

Now I sought the Absolute and Undefined of "the other side," once again. As I continued to read my Bible, I could see that this was not the path that Jesus had taken, for he would call upon Abba, the Father, to guide him, although I'm sure that he knew this to be only one aspect of our loving Source. I reframed my approach to Jesus, thinking of him as an older and wiser brother, who also wanted to embody God here in his body, and indeed he did, and I realized that he was a mentor. In Eastern terms, he was a guru or a doorway to the Divine. His Christed presence opened my mystic eyes to the meanings behind his recorded words, and this felt like companionship as I sought God, the Father, as Jesus had before me. I had no preconceived notion of the moment when I would come before God's presence as Jesus had known it, or if this would instead be just like I'd experienced in Heaven. Who knew what would happen? I was ready for anything. Ready to accept whatever happened, knowing it was untainted truth, and understanding intellectually at least, that it would be for my good.

I asked for a direct encounter, and would wait for it. I waited for months of daily practice, before something happened.

Did I mention that I had been as chaste as a spiritual celebrant since the stroke? I think not. Jonathan had stopped this aspect of our marriage, although he often blamed me for it. Quite often, one or both of us were too ill to consider it even if desire existed. Well, I was also channeling this energy of pure desire for union into my new practice, I imagine. Surely this is the energy that had buoyed many a saint up before little ignorant me. Denied of all else, one desires union like a

> Take me into your bridal chambers that I may chant with them that sing to you.
> (Manichaean Psalm Book)

thirsty man desires a drink of cool water. Isn't this what we all desire? We want completeness, wholeness, and unity with all the goodness of life, don't we?

One day, while waiting in the silence for this redemption, I sensed I was not alone in the soft darkness of the meditative state. An inrushing of loving acceptance within the velvety blackness made me aware that the larger Self that was all goodness, surrounded my small self. It felt just like it had when I was out of my body, during my near death experience! I felt suddenly whole. I felt as if I had again returned Home. I was in Its presence! Tiny me in the midst of endless space of soft and loving darkness. No, I was not separate, in a corner. I was sheltered within It, Beloved Self. I knew why others have been moved to hallelujahs and praise, for nothing more can be said or asked for when this occurs!

This was the one-with-One experience I had sought. It has been here all along, I realized! It had not shifted away from me. I had simply lost my awareness of it. Now it was back, with all the intensity of my out-of-body experience.

There was no theology necessary for me to experience the full connection I'd sought. I was un-tethered from all prior religious instruction, and free to see the truth which exists in all religions, the simple and beautiful truth seen through the eyes of mystics of all faiths.

There are endless names for God, this ineffable creator of all. Perhaps the Jews acknowledge this best, when referring to this greatness as G-d, HaShem, or YHVH. How can a name capture it? There is no way to define it, but you know it when it is encountered. It is too holy to even speak out loud. The saints of both Old Testament and New fell to their knees before it. I refer to it

> You received the Spirit of sonship. And by him we cry, "Abba," Father. The spirit himself testifies with our spirit that we are God's children. Now if we are children, then we are heirs---heirs of God and co-heirs with Christ. (Romans 8:15-17)

by many appellations, such as All That Is, the One, our Source, Abba, Divine Mind, and Our Creator, more often than using the childhood reference to God, which seems to limit it down to the old man with the beard that sits in judgment of us all. I know that it does not, but the word picture of God the Father can falsely impose limits on its greatness. Yet, this name persists because it is programmed so deeply within me and within our culture; thus, I use it for myself and for you. I now was back in touch with the indefinable infinity of goodness from which I came and to which I shall return, but was doing so within my body! And how I continually craved this state! And how, once there, I loved to dwell interminably, until in one of my sessions I sensed that there was more than silent communion being offered.

I was receiving guidance. It was soft and clear, direct and with no doubt, the truth. My truth. I was being offered more, still! This is as Jesus Christ had promised when he left this earth, saying that the Mighty Counselor, the Holy Spirit, would be there for us.

I was now experiencing that timeless union with a mighty power, an Allness, and Wholeness, and Peace. This is the prayer closet — just you and God shut off together in this secret place. And the stillness was stirring with portent for me.

Jesus said when you knock the door to the Kingdom will be opened. Also, that with faith the size of a mustard seed you can move mountains. He knew this from experience — there was something very determined and solid in his

> Do not conform any longer to the pattern of this world, but be transformed by the renewing of your mind. Then you will be able to test and approve of what God's will is---his good, pleasing, and perfect will. (Romans 12:2)

conviction and equally solid about his results. He had unshakeable knowledge, not blind faith. Perhaps this was gained during his forty days and forty nights of temptation, for he learned to lean upon God and to reject all else during this trial. He came out of this trial with a belief as solid as our knowledge that gravity will hold our feet to the crust of the Earth.

St. John knew this too, for he said when you know the truth, it will set you free. As indeed, it does. And here in this place of knowing, Spirit wanted to teach me more about this.

Insights came. Direction was given. The symbolic "fire" that is the Holy Spirit seemed to come in a rush of new ideas, sudden realizations, and in intense inner dialogue with my Higher Self or Soul or Spirit.

Spirit was becoming my companion and a teacher who corrected me daily. I entered, as St. Theresa of Avila once said, the "Inner Castle," and I learned that we can find answers both spiritual and material in that castle. I received very down-to-Earth instruction, and a remarkable sequence of events then fell into place. All these wonderful things were happening in my life, leading up to the appearance of the clerics that would occur when Jonathan's crises were peaking and he needed me.

Beginning to Move the Body

Later in Summer 2008

I ACCEPTED MY FAMILY DOCTOR'S SUGGESTION that I take physical therapy to get moving again, and by this, to possibly reverse the organ shutdown that was in progress. By now, there was no bodily system working properly, and no medication to help it.

I had become receptive and willing to take direction given during my meditations. To my surprise, I was beginning to hear Spirit telling me that "Thy will be done" didn't necessarily mean, "Okay, I guess you want me to be sick." Bending to that higher will didn't necessarily mean I must suffer, and it didn't mean that I needed to pray only for others. I had earlier learned a great lesson due to the brain stem stroke and then going to heaven. I learned that to gain myself I must lose myself. It seemed that this lesson was an involuntarily one, for who would choose to likely die? I did not realize that with this new and clear instruction to become well, that

I was about to learn this healing form of surrender again, even more deeply. Now, I was going to lose myself in order to gain myself, and it was going to be voluntary and in fact, sought beyond all else.

It began as a sequence of small things. A therapist helped me to walk for ten minutes, holding onto bars on either side of my wobbly body, while she rested her hand on the small of my back to prevent the dreaded backward flip. Following this with a few minutes on a recombinant bike, I needed heat packs and massage to lessen the pain that resulted.

After twelve weeks of therapy, I used a cane while I walked a paved trail around the pond behind my home: Five minutes of moving away from the house, and then five more straining minutes back. I breathed fresh air and looked up at the sky and across to the green grass all about me. Sometimes, I was joined by a little Sandhill crane family that would pace me as I edged around the body of water.

Back home again, I'd need my TENS unit and moist heat to recover. After a month of such effort, my therapist challenged me to increase my walk to twenty minutes. My spiritual re-connection grew apace with my stamina, thanks to inner guidance. I call this particular intersection of physical and spiritual prompting a "synchronicity." In this case, I somehow found myself in possession of a compelling description of something called walking meditation.

I believe that synchronicity is a phenomenon of life that you will recognize if it happens to you. It is a convergence of people and events in a way that brings something you desire within your grasp. Synchronicities are delightful little delivery systems that the Universe deploys to teach, to support, and to love you. Perhaps the angels take part in this, as the invisible arms and legs of the Supreme Being. The manner in which this occurs is often startling and profoundly moving. It will appear to be improbable, and remarkable, when it happens. If it did not, you would have remained waiting for a breakthrough. Because it happened, it blesses you. It feels like and is, in fact, grace.

And so, thanks to a synchronicity I learned the Buddhist practice of walking meditation. There are several types, but the one I learned suggested that I count out eight steps as I took a breath in, and another eight steps as I breathed out.

> ... when God watched over me, when his lamp shown upon my head, and by his light I walked through the darkness. (Job 29:3)

I added this to my practice while I increased to twenty minutes of movement around the pond. I found my natural rhythm was to take eight steps on my in-breath, and then ten on the out-breath. What a joy to lose myself in this! My inner peace deepened while moving within the comforting framework of this counting and the rise and fall of my chest. There was little room to think of anything else other than the movement of my feet and my cane, plus the counting of those steps in rhythm with my breath.

Amid this physical motion, an inward motion toward greater life force occurred. I heard again from Spirit, and it was clearly saying, "Understand this: God's will for you is to be whole and well and perfect, just like you were made. Spirit wishes you joy and peace and power and love, not surrender to sadness and pain."

My heart swelled as I dwelt with such thoughts. But another synchronicity was about to bring even greater teaching. . .

On a good day for Jonathan, one in which he had a bit of energy and clarity between surgeries, he suggested that we take a drive to the town just north of us. There was a book outlet there, which had opened temporarily in a vacant big box store. It would only be there until its one time inventory dwindled.

Soon we stood agape before an expansive display of books laid out on folding tables. I chose the three sections closest to the door, because I could remain standing only so long. Jonathan headed off toward the military section, as I moved toward the metaphysical section.

Before the stroke, I'd used my empathic skills to read fortunes at neighborhood parties and Psychic Fairs. Tarot Cards were useful props that seemed to elicit a stronger energetic focus from the person I was reading. I didn't need the cards myself, for I was reading the person, not the cards.

Now, before me, was a book on Tarot reading from a new perspective: "The Tarot: A Key to the Wisdom of the Ages" written by Dr. Paul Foster Case. Its focus was on the ageless wisdom contained within the symbols in the Major Arcana (the face cards which have been omitted from the ordinary playing deck) rather than on its use for divination. The book said, "Take me home." This was why I had come, and Jonathan had been the conduit for this blessing.

I soon consumed it, and wanting more, listened to lectures from the mystery school formed around Dr. Case's work. Although the roots of all mystery schools are deliberately obscured, they may have begun well before the time of Christ to amass the esoteric knowledge that was often unsafe to share. Some say that Jesus himself attended such a school during his missing years. These "sub rosa" or secret organizations carried great metaphysical truths over hundreds of years, most importantly, teaching meditation and visualization to initiates, but carrying forward the esoteric meanings of the Catholic sacraments and of the Holy Mass, as well. Remaining until the present day, such schools no longer fear persecution but remain overshadowed by more mainstream dilutions of the truth.

The lessons spoke of G-d, the Limitless Love, and I read with an inner thrill of things I had experienced on the other side. I eagerly anticipated each mailing of new material, while I continued my daily meditations at home and the walking meditations outdoors.

I AM ONE WITH THE ONE bubbled up into my consciousness and seemed to recite itself organically as my left foot contacted the Earth and I began my inhale, once my daily walk began. Where did this phrase, I AM ONE WITH THE ONE come from? I cannot explain it based on conventional thinking. It did not originate with any part of me I could identify as Emily. It simply surfaced into my consciousness, and because it felt right, I came to love the feeling I had while thinking about and mentally repeating this phrase during these solitary walks in nature, and in pauses during my studies.

I no longer felt alone, even when I was not in the meditative state. I became aware of invisible companions, guides and angels actively supporting me.

How can I describe this to you?

It began, it seemed, with my willingness to expand my awareness beyond the merely physical to sensations, much as I had when I recognized my own empathic and clairsentient and precognitive experiences. And then when I simply asked, "Is someone there?" and I received "Yes, we are here to walk with you and to guide you and to protect you," I no longer questioned that the unseen can be real.

This awareness was acute during meditation. I knew I was no longer meditating alone, one-on-One, but rather Us-in-One. And I found during meditation time that I was shifting energetically, at a soul level, from the physical space of my room to another place. Within the space of Universal Mind, I was led to a building, and then a classroom within it that was filled with wooden desks for students, and a lectern. Invited to take a seat, I attended lectures during such meditation periods.

I cannot recall what I was being taught, in order to relate it here now. What I recall, instead, is the sense of peace and the assurance I felt that I was hearing truth and that the words were sinking into my subconscious as inner knowing, and a cumulative restoration to wholeness. I also felt the camaraderie and acceptance that comes from being with like minds.

It was about this time that, while resting and thinking in my meditation room, that I yielded into an unfamiliar forgiveness toward others who had hurt me in the past. Was it because of instruction in my etheric classroom?

I saw myself, as if it were happening in the physical and not just in my mind, forgiving my adoptive mother for unspeakable abuses of me.

She had attacked me, and I could not escape her, being so small and young. I recalled the pain in my nether parts, and the fear bunching up in my solar plexus, every time that this happened. Yet, I tried now to imagine that she knew no better. She was more than my torturer. She was a fellow human being. In her actions toward me, was she repeating something that had happened to her?

This imaginary encounter with her united us as fellow victims. For the moment, there was no longer the palpable disparity between my role as a victim and hers as a perpetrator. I gained sympathy for her, and my own emotional pain seemed to melt away just a bit.

Visualization

2009

THE DISCIPLINE OF MEDITATION was more than just work. It was a joy, for it was now more rarified and efficacious than it had ever been. I spent hours a day in this state. I was ready for the next step. With weekly lessons coming by mail, and the support from the teachers of my inner classroom, I began to creatively visualize a new beginning for myself.

Although seemingly impossible, I tried anyway. I tried to imagine a life better than the one I had lived up to this point. Having no definition within myself of something better, I repeatedly failed. What I had lived was all that I knew. Other people lived better lives. It was evidently not my lot in life to live like them. I perceived weakness and faults in myself, and scant little skill or assets. I doubted my own value. And there was no hope offered from the doctors who said there was no recovery from this fatal disease I'd endured for so long. But I did not fear failure, for I was being buoyed up by unseen forces that I knew would not let me.

I continued to try. I tried to imagine seeing myself saying, "I am well," but my body, aching and unreliable, said, "No, you are not."

> But we hope for what we do not yet have, we wait for it patiently. (Romans 8:25)

My rational mind felt justified in my failure. It was so difficult to feel and see, in my mind's eye, that I was well, when my logical mind kept pointing out that the lab reports and the doctors' prognostications made clear that I wasn't.

It was impossible for me to imagine "I live a happy life," either, for I did not, save for this development of comfort within meditation and its soft extensions of peace into those periods in between sessions. Yes, I was feeling better inside through such moments of solace and communion with my inner teachers. But my *outside*, the physical hardships and the tension of life with Jonathan, was not what happiness looks like.

I couldn't imagine that I was free to do anything when in fact I was constrained within what seemed to be an iron box with chains and locks hung all around it. The restoral of logic, thanks to the rebuilding of the synapses between my right and left brain as I healed from the stroke effects, once again said emphatically that to think otherwise would be delusional. *Look at reality, not at these daydreams, you silly woman.* So I tried a different approach. . . I thought, *I am not well, certainly, but I can acknowledge that it is heartening to now have daily walks around the pond, filled with breath, invocation, and rhythmic movement that was once not possible.* I imagined, in the tiniest way, that I could do more. I looked only at the positive aspects of my life, in this temporary and tentative way, like opening a door just a crack, letting in the narrowest shaft of light. Dare I indulge in this little fantasy? Okay, call it fantasy! I had a flash in which I found myself enjoying the thought of wellness, something recalled from the past, if not now. In that brief moment, I felt it was true!

With this tiniest of shifts in my mental orientation, this narrow glint of light into the darkness, I wondered, *can I let still more light in or would this be ridiculous and pathetic?*

It was true that others would think me to be silly, perhaps, or they might even pity me for indulging in such contrary thoughts as a way to escape the pain of my reality. I resolved that not even Jonathan would know of the light of hope that was dawning within me. Exposing this would puncture, like a sputtering little rubber balloon, all of its airy dreamlike qualities and dissipate them into nothingness again. This was something to be nurtured and protected, and, like an experiment, to be allowed to develop so that I might see whether it could become concrete, or be revealed that it could not.

Having decided this, when "reality" would punch into my solar plexus with the thought that I wasn't actually well, I'd acknowledge this, but agree with myself that I would keep up my little game of imagining otherwise.

Why not try this little exercise? (Yes, I said this to myself, but why not *you*?)

I had reached the juncture of believability versus illusion. Both sides seemed to now be equally weighted, instead of all the weight being on the "illusionary" side of my inner sentiments.

Okay, ready or not, it was time to try visualizing as I had read about in my daily lessons. It was only for five minutes a few times a day, and surely my teachers had tried visualization and had succeeded, or they would not insist that I try it, too.

133

Daily, I resolved to tell no one I took excursions into fantasy, and that way I would not be made fun of, diluting the power of this growing visualization that my body was healed. I wrote down specifics about what my own wellness would look and feel like. It went something like this:

I am walking around the pond, and I pass by someone who says, "Your eyes are looking so clear and bright, and you have a spring in your step!" I imagine looking at my arms and seeing clear and rosy skin. I move to an interior view of my body while I feel my muscles and bones carrying me smoothly along. I see my entire nervous system sparking and glowing as it relays its messages with perfection. I see my circulatory system, lit up in vibrant blues and reds, carrying blood effortlessly, nourishing my cells. I see my respiratory system taking air in, using what it wishes and discarding the rest on my exhale. I see my digestive system moving food perfectly down to my stomach, drawing all the nutrients I need and distributing it out to every cell, and moving all that is left easily out of my system. I see my endocrine system, every sweet little gland, communicating back and forth in perfect harmony to keep my body running smoothly. I admire all of these various systems and imagine them all working with each other in a beautiful symphony of cooperation. All these systems, in pristine order, are making me feel wonderful inside my own skin, and my outward appearance is equally beautiful, reflecting this inner harmony and order.

And so I dwelt with these thoughts, bringing them to life with the sounds and sights and aromas and somatic feelings of wellness as I did so.

Do you think you could try this, too? Here are guidelines I can offer:

Begin by asking yourself, "What do I desire more than anything else?" Perhaps it is healing you seek, as I did, or perhaps it is something else. The field is wide open for you to define as you wish.

Are you willing to focus upon this one desire now, to the exclusion of all other desires? Okay, imagine the reality of this, as if it were already true. What are the colors? The sounds? The movement of it? Can you touch it? What does it feel like? Is there a scent associated with it? How do you feel knowing that you have what you desire?

Go over every detail of this. Write about it, in present tense. Day dream about it as if it is true and enjoy the sensations with satisfaction. Mentally, create a short video of the experience of your fulfilled desire. Play the video several times a day, seeing it through the eye of your mind, and be sure to play the video as you awaken in the morning, and as your last thought before falling asleep at night. Be grateful, be jubilant, and know in your heart that it is already in existence in the ethers. Its debut, its magical appearance in your life, is imminent. So you have cause for gratitude and thanks for what is already yours in your heart.

I hope that with practice you will come to enjoy this respite from "reality," as I did. It may bring you much more than respite, for dreams can and do come true.

I performed my own healing visualization several times a day, running it in my mind's eye, and imagining that I was by-passing my physical eyes but sending just as an effective signal to the brain's vision center (the medulla oblongata) as physical sight. I imagined that my mental signals were being accepted, and that this input went to those higher parts of the brain that would recognize the input as reality.

It was so enjoyable to imagine being well, that I not only did this exercise as I've instructed you to do, but I added extra sessions. I

135

thought, if three times a day is good, then four or five times should be even better.

Then, I was occasionally lifted up into joyful reverie between these sessions; I received little glimpses of this altered reality spontaneously peeking through the clouds of my mind.

While steady in my course of daily visualization, my journal (something I've kept since childhood) recorded more than the course of my life and my actions. Its entries were filled with self-recrimination. And like in the days before the stroke, I still had a fear of fear itself. I suspected this fear was deeper than my conscious thoughts and visualizations could reach.

I believed that deep within, perhaps in my subconscious, I must be undeserving of happiness. Although I was happy during visualizations, and had glimmers of success between these practice sessions, my overall thoughts were negative. I often had panic and stabs to my heart after embracing my positive visions. *Would I ever stop the hurtful rebukes my mind would throw up to me after I embraced a positive dream?* I wondered if I could I ever break this pattern, to live a life beyond the fear that crippled me.

Another synchronicity occurred, in answer to my frustration. A dream study group was forming in town. Dreams could be the way to peer through into my subconscious belief system! Perhaps if I could map out its sad beliefs, I could then figure out how to stop it.

I became a member of the group, and was soon recording three or four dreams every night. On Wednesdays, we'd share our week of dreams, and offer insights to each other about the symbols and the substance of each of them. In my case, the dreams were disturbing and the symbols were beyond comprehension.

Then the thought came during meditation, as if this was personal instruction: When you go to sleep, tell your subconscious to be very clear and to use easily understood symbols.

This instruction continued: I was to ask my subconscious to advise me and guide me, and trust it to bring me guidance from Universal Consciousness. The surprising guidance continued: Your subconscious is smart, and it works for you because it IS you. Both the challenges and the successes that you experience are good. They are to be welcomed, not feared.

In learning that visualization is a way to instruct the subconscious to bring goodness to me, and then learning I was sabotaging myself because some existing understandings that my subconscious held were not helpful although it truly thought that they were, I thought, *how can I ever beat this? The programming is so powerful it pulls me back from success relentlessly. It doesn't want me to succeed.*

Journaling and dream analysis was a start in understanding the nature of the beast, as I still thought the subconscious to be. I remained distrustful of it, yet hopeful that it would take my direction through the positive visual images I now offered as frequent feedings.

A dream recorded at that time reveals my ambivalence:

I was traveling in a sort of long basket, floating in water. A man was the head of a group of fellow travelers, like me. I joined the group and tended a little gray cat. She had stuff in her mouth that I swept out. Then she trusted me to help her empty out all kinds (big and small) of stuff she'd swallowed that was now making her ill. She had her own little white plastic basket she didn't always stay in. Then I spoke to the man who was leading us travelers. I said to him, "I don't know how

137

you can ever recover from so much pain," and I hugged him. During the dream I had an impression that when we hugged we merged---we were really one soul.

It was through dreams, such as this one, that I came to acknowledge the vulnerable aspects of my soul, particularly in the image of the little gray cat who needed so many things swept out of her before she could heal. I also retained the awareness, so vividly given during my near death experience, that we are never alone, and that we can choose to elevate ourselves from sadness through expressing love for others. In fact, it is a common energy field of benevolence, in which we all swim. The sea of universal subconscious is not to be feared, for there is also love that overcomes all. If only my subconscious believed this enough to allow my life to change!

Relocation for a New Start

Later in 2009
On the way to Arizona

ONE DAY, DURING MY WALKING MEDITATION, I felt inner guidance suggest that we move away from Florida to Arizona.

I daydreamed about it, but would we have the physical ability to move ever again? I had long been too ill, and coupled with Jonathan's condition, it wasn't realistic. He had, by this time, undergone all three neck surgeries, and he was weak both physically and mentally. No longer playing softball, he rested day and night in a fog of pain medications. He needed help with most everything, and it didn't seem safe for him to leave the house by himself anymore.

Why would I receive such a suggestion? Well, I could now walk outdoors in the sunlight, and my mental focus had improved because of meditation. Listening to the inner voice, and having a newfound sense that someone or something loved me and was looking out for me, I considered this impulse to perhaps be higher self prompting, not just fodder for daydreaming.

As I continued to entertain such thoughts, I realized that were I to move, no one in my new location would know that I was sick. And I could pretend whenever out with others, that I was not.

What a concept! I would no longer be surrounded by people who believed that I was very ill and would soon die.

Surely, I blamed no one for thinking this. Without doubt, it had taken tolerance, even courage, to be in a room with me as I teetered, coughed uncontrollably, and lapsed into silence when it became too challenging to talk. If *I* couldn't see myself healing, how could *they* be expected to see me well? Leaving this environment could only help my visualization. It would be worth the effort to move. And I would "fake" wellness once I was in my new surroundings.

When I ventured to speak about this with Jonathan, it amazed me to hear that he shared my interest in moving. He didn't know about my visualization practice, or of my plan to fake being well, of course. But my feeling that there was something good and benevolent looking out for me only increased when I learned that for some time prior to his surgeries, Jonathan had been researching this very move himself.

He knew of the perfect locale for us and asked me to work with a real estate agent that had been sending him MLS listings from there for months! Soon after, we flew to Arizona to scout out our new home. Jonathan was fragile, and his focus drifted in and out, but he worked hard at being present to what was occurring now. We leaned on each other, and made it happen. I asked my guides and angels to kindly protect us, and we received this. Purchasing a little home that matched our shared vision, Jonathan and I then returned to Florida. We'd need to sell our home there, before we could return to our little condo in the desert.

I found myself in conflict, regarding what to visualize. I felt I could focus well on just one desire at a time. Which desire was more important? Should I focus upon my health or the move? Well, I thought, *which would be easier to believe in?* The move, of course. This was because a successful move was much more believable than trying to reject reality by seeing myself well. And so, I focused my creative thinking only on selling the home.

> For he will command his angels concerning you to guard you in all your ways; they will lift you up in their hands, so that you will not strike your foot against a stone. (Psalm 91:11-12)

I now trusted more than ever upon my inner guidance. In fact, because I was coming to think that I had an actual guide or guides helping me along, and angels who loved me, I asked my guides and angels to hold the focus of making me well, as my proxies, until I could resume this. How comforting it was to have such confidence in God's helpers now! This allowed me to develop a "home sale" visualization that went something like this:

I see our buyers walking up the path into the screened courtyard and through the front door of our home. They are exploring each room, with increasing glee at the thought that they will soon be living here. I now see a ten foot wide rubber stamp directed by my thoughts alone. The stamp moves through the air to imprint, with a satisfying thump, the word SOLD on each and every wall of the home. I am moving now, in my mind's eye, from room to room, stamping each wall. Then I move up like a bird and soar over the house. From there, I look down onto the rooftop where I see a huge neon sign lit up in glitzy colors, just like Las Vegas, virtually shouting out to our neighbors the joyous word SOLD, and with a huge dollar sign, the amount it sold for. Fireworks splash iridescent greens and pinks in the night sky over this exuberant display.

I focused intently upon this visualization in five minute stretches several times a day. From day to day, the visualization became ever more colorful, noisier, and more energetic. After a few weeks of such practice, I felt, as I played it over in my mind like a video, that it was inevitable it would become a reality.

I was not perfect at this, by any means. My periods of excitement and hopefulness were plagued by periodic stabs to my oft-abused heart and solar plexus. I then criticized myself for holding such fantasies as my only strategy for selling a house in a period when nothing was selling in the neighborhood, or anywhere in the country, because of an economic downturn.

It was not natural or easy, but I had discipline now. Whenever I had attacks of doubt, therefore, I re-centered myself back onto my visualization practice. I asked myself, *Are there any alternatives to continuing my practice? If there is nothing else I can do, and it does no harm to try, do it anyway.* So I told no one, avoiding the disempowering embarrassment that might ensue, and continued the practice. Although it took longer than I had imagined it would, in time we received a purchase offer from a couple who had walked up that path into the house where they did indeed whisper first, and then speak aloud, of how much they loved the home.

"We don't want a thing about it to change! Can we buy your furnishings, too?" said the bearded beekeeper from New Hampshire, his words overlapping those of his wife.

Agreeing to this and a short close date, the burden of a cross-country move was easily lightened and we were soon on our way. Because the physical manifestation of my home sale visualization was even better than I had imagined, my confidence grew. This technique works! My new reality was a mirror of what I had focused my thoughts and feelings upon, but this mirror had even more inherent goodness and joy than I had built into the images I'd embraced.

With this experiment, I had a better understanding of how manifestation works. I was working with "cause" instead of cause's "effect." My inner guides and angels had given me the ability to keep trying until I got it. Through the feelings and beliefs I'd generated with my visualization, I'd created an energetic framework that physical reality could mimic. Houses placed on the market eventually sell, but this particular sale had details I'd included in the visualization that were quite unique.

I began to notice that whatever I clearly visualize always appears in my reality. The timing on this varies. It might be instantaneous when I don't care much about the outcome and use a light touch regarding the matter. I observe delays when it is difficult to stretch my mind and wholeheartedly believe and feel what I'm depicting in visualization. This even happens with repeated unintentional daydreams or worries. When the results aren't as good as or better than what I've written into my mental video, it skews the results in a way that reflects my fears or lack of belief in the law.

At the time after the home sale, I continued experimenting with inconsequential things, and saw that the more joyful and confident and grateful I was, the more I saw things as if they'd already happened, the easier it worked. With newfound confidence, I returned to working with the biggest visualization of all: SEEING MYSELF WELL.

In Arizona I kept my illness a secret. No one knew how dire my diagnosis was or how poorly I felt. Since Jonathan chose not to acknowledge it either, I knew that the only talk about my health from that point forward would be during doctor appointments. This was simply perfect.

I still leaned on a cane, but no longer required a wheelchair. I could feign wellness for the short stretches of time when I was with others in our neighborly community. If, out of curiosity or concern, someone asked about my cane, I joked about it, saying simply that I "liked the look." Better they thought I was eccentric than ill!

My meditations and study took place in an easy chair in the den I shared with Jonathan. I spent all morning with this work, often listening to binaural beats in the brainwave frequency of Alpha or Alpha-Gamma as I studied. When I meditated, I deepened my descent into the soft darkness by switching to a Delta brainwave frequency, using ear buds for this. While the sounds acted upon my subconscious, they also created a permeable sound barrier for the inner work I was doing. If Jonathan needed me, I would still hear it.

> The tongue has the power of life and death, and those who love it will eat its fruit. (Proverbs 18:21)
>
> And God said, "Let there be light, and there was light." (Genesis 1:3)
>
> The eye is the lamp of the body. If your eyes are good, your whole body will be full of light. (Matthew 6:22)

I again had to drive, although I went out rarely. Otherwise, I was home, concentrating on Jonathan who was even less focused mentally since we'd moved. He needed daily supervision and help with bathing, dressing, and eating. Once his rally during our move subsided, he could do little more than watch TV and silently gaze out the windows to the mountains that edged the valley.

Like a good sister to my spiritual brother, I cared for him.

Experiments Lead to Knowledge

Christmas, 2009

I CONTINUED LEARNING THE CRAFT of working with cause rather than with effect. My early experiments had taught me to ignore what I was experiencing in the moment unless it exceeded my heart's every desire. Not that I could always do this. . . it was a struggle. But I was learning to pay attention to what I was thinking, feeling, and seeing in my mind's eye. My inner sight, another form of my inner word, was to be protected above all else. What I focused upon and felt in that vibrant world of my own creation, within the vibration of my mental and somatic focus, occasionally delighted me. I was becoming mindful of my thoughts, and learning to rein them in when they buzzed off into negativity.

It had dawned on me based on close observation of my thoughts and outcomes, that all the power of the Universe, in this microcosm of my mind, compelled what I "saw" to become real. My confidence accelerated each time I disciplined myself to do this imaginative work of seeing happy outcomes. When I could hold the reins tightly enough, my goal manifested just as I saw it, or better.

My technique was inconsistent, but I had succeeded often enough to understand that this "cause," my imaginative focus, would create the pleasing "effect" that would take place in the future. What love Source has for us, to have made us

> But when he asks he must believe and not doubt, because he who doubts is like a wave of the sea, blown and tossed by the wind. (James 1:6)

creators, like Him, welcoming us to sit at His right hand, so to speak, in the Heavens, next to our brother Jesus the Christ. As Jesus had said to us, we will do as much and even more than He did, and he promised that the faith amounting to a little mustard seed was the beginning of what could become a great tree. I had learned to create through the inner guidance and the loving direction that had been given me after I called out to God with all my heart to make Himself known to me, and the subsequent direction I'd received to "see myself well."

To make this very clear, I'm not saying that it isn't hard work to change one's beliefs, to ignore the input of the senses, and the plans one's logical mind might suggest in lieu of working with "cause." Constant correction is required. It is very much like meditation, in which one continually brings the mind gently back to the stillness whenever it wanders. When you intend to manifest something, you must pay attention to the conscious thought process, and gently bring yourself back to the desired thought rather than what the *mind* says is reality. This is how we work with the greatest truth which is a law of love. For surely we are loved, to have been given this privilege to pursue our desires in growing our way back to God.

My meditations supplied ongoing direction, but the disciplining of my mind was up to me. I had such a sense of responsibility as I quietly and secretly did this work! I felt the power in it continue to grow as I kept my silence.

One of my first discoveries with visualization had to do with the plausibility of my mental images, as I have already alluded to. I found that I could not imagine that visualization could immediately cure MF. At the same time that I could imagine that I was well, I realized that I could only imagine incremental improvements leading to this, not a lightning flash change to wellness.

It may seem silly, but my logical mind could not compute what would happen if I stopped taking the blood altering medication, interferon, before there was empirical evidence that I was well. My logical mind said that stopping this drug before I was cured, held the risk I'd quickly deteriorate to a point where I'd stroke out or hemorrhage. But what if I continued to take my medications when I'd had a sudden cure I wasn't yet aware of? The over-medication would surely harm me, as well.

What I could believe, and continue to feel safe with, was this: From one blood test to the next, I would see a slight improvement. Each test would show fewer signs of disease, warranting a modest reduction in medication. Perhaps it would take a recurring pattern of reduced signs of disease, over the course of months, before my doctor would reduce the medication, but everything would happen in slow motion while keeping me safe. Because my medication dosages were high, it would take several iterations of this before I was off of it, but this was a vision I could believe in, and one that my logical mind would not fear. *Not all at once, but a little at a time . . .* this was a vision I could comfortably and plausibly accept. I had discovered a durable template for change, when the change seems too extreme to believe. This is a magical formula that can work for anyone, I think. Try it yourself, if your goal seems too daunting to be achievable.

When I realized this, my visualizations became less fantastical to me, and more realistic. I became excited about this plan, knowing that for me, it was much better than asking for a miracle to occur instantly. I knew that the change would come in this manner, for I could comfortably believe in it.

It was tempting to work out the steps that would lead to the full manifestation of wellness. I knew not to use my logical mind to map it all out, dictating to the Universe just how it would look. Understanding only a bit about the way that the subconscious mind works, I knew that my job was not visualizing how to get from Point A to Point B in this or any other manifestation. My only job was to feel and believe in the visualization as if it had already occured, and to avoid undermining myself afterwards with negativity.

When I noticed less neuropathy, I rejoiced. Here was evidence that I was beginning to conform to my inner vision. I had not specified in my "video" that neuropathy would go away first, nor how it would go away, but it had. The drop in pain was recent, and I could probably explain some variance in the pain level away, so I would not consider telling others that I'd been healed by applying Universal Law. Who, in my world, even knew that such Law existed? No one. To try to explain would likely require defense of my new knowledge, and I might feel silly for doing such things when my detractors felt I should be focused instead on a medical cure.

And what a mess I was, as I plodded along, just me and God and my troupe of angels and guides. I continued working the plan with seeing myself well, and experimenting with lesser, day-to-day concerns. I learned more about myself. For the first time, I looked at myself honestly and had to say that my natural frame of mind was negative, and I couldn't hold my focus on a positive outcome. I just didn't believe life could be positive. Not for me. This wasn't just my conscious expectation, it was my subconscious layered with decades of reinforcement.

Still taking my first steps of faith, my thoughts and feelings vacillated incessantly. I tried and failed much more often than I succeeded, in my attempts to hold a belief in a positive outcome for virtually any issue in my life. I failed in spite of having proof positive that what I was doing works! I felt there must be something wrong with me, for why was I unable to do this? I bounced back and forth between success and failure, beaten incessantly by my own negative thoughts. I hated the inner critic preventing my success, which said *don't be such a silly woman. This won't work.* Even when I told this voice to stop, or tried to ignore it, it persisted. In fact, pushing it away seemed only to make it stronger. Is this what a schizophrenic feels like, resisting the darkness?

Seeing that I sabotaged myself through my own disbelief, I wrote about this phenomenon repeatedly in my journal, with increasing frustration. Understanding my dreams wasn't enough! Every day I recorded what I was working on through visualization, and my results. I tried to capture the details of my inner battle, hoping that by bringing it to light, I'd gain insights that would lead to peace.

I had a desire to record what I was being taught, as well. Having invited the presence of all the benevolent guides and angels who wanted to help me day and night, and especially during meditation, I'd write about my interactions with them, too. With some reluctance to admit this even to myself, I recorded how I had developed a relationship with an amusing person or entity that was no longer in a body, but had often been in a body at the same time I had been, in prior incarnations. He told me we had been friends and fellow physicians in prior lives on a planet other than Earth, and that I should never refer to him as a guide. He said, "I am your friend, and I admire you for deciding to do this — to incarnate onto Earth. I wouldn't have done it!" I had to believe this mention of other lives, because I'd already studied the sausage-making which led to the versions of the Bible we have today, and I knew that most all of the references to reincarnation that had once been there were later removed, withholding part of the great truth from us. But there are other ways to research and confirm the veracity of this, no matter that the Bible was corrupted in this regard. You can find references to this within all of the holy books, not only the Bible. And I say "thank heavens" that reincarnation is a part of the divine plan, for this gives us endless chances to get it right!

On one occasion, during meditation, I invited my friend to join me in my body, and he did so. He didn't last long at all, exclaiming, "It's so HEAVY!" After this, we agreed that he would continue to walk with me and help whenever I asked, but he had no interest in experiencing the earth vibration again. He would be my companion, and if I needed this, would call in legions of others, too, so there would always be someone who had expertise to bear. He offered to help, or bring help, and assured me that I was never alone. He often amused me, and was tickled himself, as things developed. He would chuckle at a success, and commiserate with me at a temporary defeat, as I dwelt with my visualizations. It was delightful to have him as a witness and coach, considering I could share this with no one else without risk.

In my journal, I also recorded the arrival of an angel who called herself "Giggles." What a ridiculous and undignified name, I thought. It embarrassed me to have to record her name after learning it during a meditation when I invited those who had an interest in my spiritual growth to identify themselves. What did she want to help me with? To be joyful. To laugh. To be lighthearted about what I was doing. To feel happiness without cause.

How could I be joyful when the battle between my conscious desires and my subconscious programming had never seemed more glaringly incalcitrant? Logically, negative disbelief surely hurt me, and *I was an adult now, fully in charge of my will, with a better idea now of how to apply it, so let's just stop it,* I told myself. I tried to believe that over time I could stop it, but the inner critic was mighty. I felt weak and broken.

Inner Vision Changes Outcomes

2010

IN SPITE OF THIS, I PERSISTED in this mental and sensate practice of seeing myself well, during walks on a nature trail close to my new home. Lined with mature trees, manicured shrubs, and desert flowers, I felt energetic points along the path, and realized there was power radiating from somewhere. It was from what I soon called the Mother Trees. Making sure no one saw, I stopped at each of these laying my hands on their rough bark, even placing my back against them, to take in more of their strength.

They were saying, "We've been here a long time, through the changes of season, building of houses, paving the road and trail, and have stood still while the sun beat down on us, the wind tore at our leaves, and lightning struck our branches. We're scarred and we've lost limbs to the forces of weather or the whimsy of man, but still we stand. Our roots go deep into this soil, and we draw from a water table invisible to those of you who walk the ground's surface.

We hear each other, and we comfort each other, sympathizing when a sapling child is lost, or winter bares us to our bones. We have enough strength to let you draw from us whenever you wish, child of man! Spend time with us, and we'll teach you how to be strong like us!"

With such greatness drawn from the deep of the Earth radiating outward from each tree, I continued my visualizations, as I walked. Even though conflicted, I persisted in holding the vision of wellness, playing it over regularly in my mind when I awoke in the morning, and when I lay my head down at the end of a day.

Even with these imperfect efforts, I observed results! I found that I could stop taking one and then another medication. The need for prescriptions dropped away, a few at a time, as symptoms disappeared. I stopped the pills used to control my blood pressure and the acidity of my stomach and ended my long dependence upon the gabapentin I'd leaned on to reduce the neuropathy that had shocked and burned me for so long.

The muscle and bone pain also diminished, and I found that I could meditate even more deeply thanks to the easing of these distractions. Physical pain is like the loud crackling heard when one is between stations on the radio dial. When that static is stopped, or even just diminished from its former volume, one can hear the broadcast clearly. It is so with pain and meditation. When the static is gone, the broadcast comes through unimpeded.

When taking Jonathan on one of our sad excursions to his doctors, we would pass a chiropractic office. Its signage indicated that there were alternative approaches to allopathic medicine practiced there. I had clung to allopathic guidance from traditional MDs and DOs, as if they were life preservers in a treacherous sea, and so I wondered as I passed this office, if it was safe to let go for even a moment. But it seemed more tantalizing every time I passed by. It beckoned me.

A logical opportunity to enter appeared when walking became too painful to continue. I'd seen a podiatrist for plantar fasciitis, caused by walking with my cane. I was more of a triped than a biped because of this extra "limb" that kept me from toppling. An inner voice that said, "Don't let him operate on you," made alternatives appealing. My first visit to the chiropractor involved being bent and pulled into sometimes painful positions, but after five sessions the foot cramp was gone. Although starting on the muscles and nerves in my foot and ankle, he ended up moving to my calves and then thighs, tracing the twists that caused pain up further and further, until we had reached the alignment of my head upon my shoulders.

During our visits we talked, and he offered color therapy to work on some "other problems." He asked me to wear sunglasses he lifted from a case that included lenses of every color of the rainbow, and while I wore the glasses, he would state affirmations which I supposed related to each color. The affirmations were about fear and abandonment. After one of these color treatments, he asked me to read a book called "Feelings Buried Alive Never Die. . ." by Karol K. Truman.

Her book begins by asking, "Have you ever felt as if there was a time bomb inside you ready to explode at any second, yet you were unable to identify the source of this feeling?" It went on, "Have you ever had the feeling of being two (or more) separate individuals or of being someone totally different than yourself – wondering who the REAL you was or where the real you had gone? Have you ever had the feeling that you were two enemies (or more) who were constantly fighting each other – as if there was a war going on inside you?" The author posited, "You could be suffering from unresolved, repressed and suppressed negative feelings you thought you had taken care of – feelings you thought were dead and gone. . . In other words, unresolved feelings buried alive never die."

The notion that I had buried my feelings seemed quite plausible. How else could I have entered the adult world, supported myself and created some semblance of peace and joy in my life during the period before the stroke and temporary departure from this physical world? I had moved from a childhood home that felt unsafe, lived in my car and then a succession of communes, before I earned enough income to feed and house myself. This hardly qualified as stability, and I had no time to look back until I was fully secure.

Ms. Truman writes, "DIS-EASE in any form is the natural consequence of unresolved negative feelings that have seemingly been forgotten, ignored or buried. . . it seems that part of us – our Higher Intelligence – is crying out to be liberated from untold years of suppression and denial." Even more stunning, "When our state of mind is one that is occupied with fears, doubts, troubles and concerns – then fears, doubts, troubles and concerns are what we naturally project outward."

Good heavens, I thought. Although I am consciously working with creation, there is that other dreaded aspect of myself that most definitely is working against me. *I hate my subconscious! And I fear it even more than I hate it!* The war within me was legitimate, and I believe I am not alone in this. Which was the stronger: My entrenched subconscious beliefs or the positive visions I intended to supplant them with?

When I acknowledged the intensity of emotions sabotaging me, it was too much! My heart was breaking, and I feared fear itself, and this old pattern was repeating itself as I once before had done. There was such explosiveness that I feared a direct look at them. They'd overpower me! Yet, they stood in the breach between the lovely imaginary world I sought to materialize, and the world in which I was living. Dis-ease was their expression.

With this fear unaddressed, so I thought, another book came my way through a friend. Called "Energy Medicine," its author, Donna Eden, sees the energy within and around the physical body, and re-directs these energies to bring about healing. Within allopathic or Western medicine, we routinely take measurement of the energy within the body through EKGs and EEGs, yet otherwise ignore the body's energy field. My medical doctors were not treating the totality of me, but I now had the knowledge to treat myself. I developed a personal energy routine drawn from Donna Eden's work, and started my day with this, as a prelude to my morning studies and meditation.

This led to my taking a course in Tai Chi, leaving Jonathan for a few hours once a week, to do so. I then experienced my own chi, or energy flow, like an invisible ball that formed between my hands when I slowly drew them apart from each other. Proof of my own energy field made my morning energy medicine routine even more meaningful.

Learning that essential oils of plants were distillations of their energy, and that a mere few drops of such oil carried vibrational healing qualities, I sprayed the air around me with them. I also applied a few drops on myself when I thought of it, particularly lavender, to calm myself.

Now curious and open, when exploring a health food store, I noticed another collection of small brown glass bottles near the essential oils. Called "Bach Remedies," a little booklet explained that these were distillations of flowers found to energetically interact with our emotions to ease fear and psychic pain. Perhaps this would help me on those days when care giving was especially unpredictable and stressful? Perhaps it would help when I felt poorly about myself because I wasn't doing well enough with my visualization work? Thinking it was worth trying, I created formulations of Bach Remedies tailored to help the emotional conditions I resonated most with, as I looked through the booklet's descriptions. This helped, too.

I discovered the books of Caroline Myss, who also spoke about the energy body. A medical intuitive, she "sees" illness's energetic signature, and describes it in clinical terms to doctors, particularly to Norman Shealy, MD, a rare physician who gave credence to her assertions that we are more than mechanical physical contraptions to be repaired like cars. He believed her when she asserted that we have energy bodies, as well, and that by treating this, the physical body will respond. She not only sees the energetic signature of disease, she sees stored emotions! Here was a confirmation of what I had read in Karol Truman's book.

I thought then about Lynne McTaggart's books, in which I learned that each human energy field is a component of a larger field that connects us all. This was why, as an empath, I sensed the emotions and thoughts of others. We overlap! Gregg Braden's books elaborated on this, most notably in his book, "The Divine Matrix." The concept of a matrix meshed perfectly with what I had experienced on the other side. There is oneness, or a unified field, to "all that is."

As I explored these new concepts and healing modalities, I continued with the old and familiar. I visualized daily, sometimes hourly. Wanting to refine techniques and increase faith, in spite of my subconscious barriers, I used the work of Shakti Gawain, Valerie Wells, and Evelyn M. Monahan, to find new ways to amplify my visualizations.

I also rediscovered a book in my home library, the famous Louise Hay classic, "You Can Heal Your Life." I'd received this book as a gift from a friend years ago, but it did not resonate with me then, and in fact had upset me upon first reading it. My initial reaction to it had been *she doesn't know what I'm going through physically--- what audacity to say that I've created this illness.* How we can change over time! Now the book looked like pure genius, and I took each remaining symptom I was experiencing, and looked them up in the index to create a paragraph full of statements. I memorized this series of affirmations, and repeated them over and over as I walked, transporting these statements of truth into my psyche, a magic elixir created just for me.

Positive momentum had built. As is often the case with spiritual growth, we struggle until a plateau is reached. We rest at that plateau. Although it may seem that we have become stagnant, we are actually being restored, and made ready for the next struggle upwards. Now resting in the comfort of affirmations which strengthened me, I was preparing for a dynamic spurt of growth toward wholeness. Since I had called out to God, sitting in expectant silence, I had received an influx of love and of guidance. I had seen improvements, and above all else the closeness with God that I'd asked for, had been given. Physical and spiritual healing was in process. Now, the mental healing was about to begin.

Forgiveness: The Door to Healing

Later in 2010

I ENTERED IN MY JOURNAL:

I want to leave my past forever and live a vital and productive and joyous life. I am still feeling that although I am told that I must forgive my parents, that this is wrong. This is the reason why I am still numb to love.

How can I say I forgive without also saying that I am meaningless? If I have been abused, denigrated, and frightened for my life since conception and through my entire formative years, hiding in my locked bedroom and frantically attempting to read the unspoken signs of danger in my parents' body language, how can I forgive this when they feel that they did nothing wrong and have never asked for forgiveness of me?

They never said that I was worthy of love and that they were sorry that they had not. . . . I am left with the perception that I am indeed not worth anything to them or thus to myself. To say that it was all right and that I can now move on – this is a lie. Its insincerity settles as bone marrow malformations into my hip bones and circulates   as   deformed teardrop cells and immature cells of all types within my blood system. It blocks my tear ducts so that I will not cry. It thumps my heart irregularly as my autonomic system joins into the silent scream for acknowledgement. I AM WORTHY. I SHOULD NOT HAVE BEEN TREATED THIS WAY.

My blood pressure rises as the entire circulatory system shrinks and squeezes as though to flee from danger. And the stab to my gut when I am hit with panic just as I slip into dreamland in the evening! My subconscious knows it is in danger and that it is considered not worth protecting, while my conscious mind maintains incorrectly that all is well and "grow up" and face the challenges of life with courage and take it no matter what is done to you.

> You have heard it was said, "Love your neighbor and hate your enemy." But I tell you: Love your enemies and pray for those who persecute you, that you may be sons of your Father in heaven. He causes his sun to rise on the evil and the good, and sends rain on the righteous and the unrighteous. If you love those who love you, what reward will you get? . . . Be perfect, therefore, as your heavenly Father is perfect. (Matthew 5:43-48)

This affects my ability to love myself and therefore love others, my ability to trust, my ability to see that my own needs are met, and my inner peace of mind. They freeze me in a permanent state of immaturity – forever a frightened and needy child.

A simple "I forgive you" does not bring about the necessary release. I have conducted acts of forgiveness so very many times throughout the years, and have reinforced this by lovingly taking care of Mom, who became so frightened of me, and rejected me when she became senile.

And how can I forgive my birth mother, who conceived me in a moment of passion, then regretted the act and selfishly hid my existence? A mother who never even informed my father of my existence? A mother who kept her

*existing child but hated me and gave me up once J slipped from her womb?
Never held me to her heart? Left my ears ringing with her thought of hate
and anger still directed toward me because J jeopardized her upcoming
marriage to a man who would make her life secure? While J, her child, was
abandoned to the orphanage? Left me so frightened of the life J saw that
my eyes crossed and began their myopic retreat into my skull when J was
only a kindergartener?*

*My saying that J forgive her does not settle my blood or my bones or rectify
a self-image to "normalcy" when J haven't even been provided with an example
by birth or adoptive parents of what this might be. And J cannot birth and
nurture myself if J am told that J am worthless.*

Coming across a book by Sue Gerhardt, "Why Love Matters:
How Affection Shapes a Baby's Brain," I learned how the earliest
relationships shape a baby's nervous system and how the pathways
formed in my brain affected my adulthood. It wasn't weakness of
character that caused me, as an adult, to be fearful of fear itself.
Neuroscience, biochemistry, and psychology substantiate the lasting
consequences of growing up in fear and self-denigration.

I was raised in a cortisol-laden soup, with a permanently triggered
HPA axis that still affected my adult brain. In plain English, this
meant my fuse was always lit. It had been so since floating in my
mother's amniotic fluid, and I was permanently on the edge of
explosion. How could my body ever rest and recover? Sadly, as Sue
reported, "the baby's vulnerability to mishandling can start even
earlier, in the womb. . . the stress response is already forming within
the developing foetus. . . in particular, high cortisol could pass
through the placenta into the [baby's] brain."

Formed in the womb and reinforced by my orphanage
beginnings, I moved to the dysfunctional and dangerous world of
my adoptive parents. I seemed to be hard-wired to fear the worst,

and in response, to live my life using control and manipulation to protect myself from harm in my frightful environment. My shaky foundation had consequences that, to paraphrase Sue's work, included self-hatred, unfulfilled love, the necessity to deny pain because I was a prisoner in my childhood household, and became a master at splitting off my feelings.

After reading Sue's work, I understood how it had happened, but despaired realizing my life approach was formed even before my birth, and was ground in deeply by a lifetime of repetition. I could only continue to trust I was being led by my Higher Self to a lasting healing. There would be pain in facing my old programming, with eyes fully open, but I believed that I was being protected and led.

Grappling with this, in meditation and in cries to God and the angels, I then was led to more information. Alice Miller, the author of "The Body Never Lies," explains in her introduction that. . . "Frequently, physical illnesses are the body's response to permanent disregard of its vital functions. One of our most vital functions is an ability to listen to the true story of our own lives." Further, "Only when I allowed myself to feel the emotions pent up for so long inside me did I start extricating myself from my own past. . . My aim was to be loved as a daughter. But the effort was all in vain. In the end I had to realize that I cannot force love to come if it is not there in the first place. On the other hand, I learned that a feeling of love will establish itself automatically once I stop demanding that I feel such love and stop obeying the moral injunctions imposed on me [by the Fourth Commandment: Thou shalt honor thy mother and thy father]. But such a sensation can happen only when I feel free and remain open and receptive to all my feelings, including the negative ones. . . I cannot manipulate my feelings."

We need "the unconditional love that our parents withheld from us. To make this happen, we need one special experience: the experience of love for the child we once were. Without it, we have no way of knowing what love consists of."

It was clear that I had sublimated a lifetime of unprocessed feelings in my body. My dear body, to protect my mind from what I could not bear, took on the burdens that manifest as dire illness. My body was so heavy with unbearable feelings that it too was foundering. Nor could I love myself, angry that I had not been loved by anyone else, and sensing perhaps I wasn't worth love. I was sick, per the medical professionals, unto death, for in spite of my visualizations, my reality had not yet changed. Per my doctors, blood cancer was soon to kill me.

I continued to meditate and trust in spite of this, and when I attended a brief class in a moment away from care giving, mention was made of a technique called tapping, purported to be helpful in freeing trapped emotions. When I got home from the class, I looked this up online and found a recording of a tapping session, which I transferred to my MP3 player to listen to during my next walk.

EFT, short for Emotional Freedom Technique, is done by thinking about a troublesome event or sensation, while tapping upon the points used in acupuncture. Information on EFT is widely available on the internet, but for clear understanding I would like to refer you to the written work of Dawson Church, Ph.D., "The Genie in Your Genes" and most recently "Mind to Matter: the Astonishing Science of How Your Brain Creates," as well as "The EFT Manual" by Gary Craig.

I soon had something to tap about: Jonathan was disoriented and argumentative, as was often the case. Initially, I contained my anger, which then changed to frustration. I felt stymied because I could not communicate with him. He was unreachable, trapped in a place where very little made sense to him, and he was likely turning outward in his anger about this. I tapped, "Even though I'm frustrated and angry about Jonathan's outbursts, I still deeply love and approve of myself." Gosh, did this ever feel awkward. Yet, I initially rated my feelings at a ten, or the worst possible, and found that after a few rounds of tapping, my feelings had dropped to a four. Once again a channel for love, Jonathan's behavior fell into context and I wanted only to help him without concern for what he might do to me in return.

Just like my experiments with visualization, this experiment with tapping worked! I used "The EFT Manual" to develop a plan of action. I decided to follow its "Personal Peace Procedure" no matter where it took me. Taking this into meditation, I got an intuitive confirmation that this energetic cleansing was blessed, and that I would have legions of angels all around me, beaming love and support, no matter how frightening things became.

The Procedure requires that you write at least fifty of the most bothersome specific events you can remember. I soon had written over eighty! I gave each event a title, as though it were a mini-movie. The instructions said to take one event from the top ten per day. I couldn't wait, and as soon as I finished with one event I moved on to the next in a blitzkrieg that lasted three days. I used every moment available during Jonathan's long morning and afternoon naps.

When I tapped on a "top ten" event, I found that my initial round of tapping would reveal feelings that had not been plain at the outset. I then recalled more events, and I saw that I often repeated the same emotional or physical injury: Only the characters changed. The play was always the same. I realized that I had lived my life attracting and manifesting that which I was used to! I added each repetitive event that came to mind to my ever-growing list. I soon had over a hundred incidents, each as their own mini-movie, to tap through.

Tears ran down my cheeks as I tapped, *I was abandoned, there is no one to comfort me and no one comes when I cry.* I tapped, I *have no one to look out for me and I don't trust people when they say that they will protect me.* My heart breaking, I tapped, *why didn't the covers pulled over my head protect me?*

I dealt with memories that had stuck with me over the years, that I'd dealt with in every which way, and had done my best to release, knowing intellectually that my adoptive mother and father were damaged and could do no better. My mind understood, but the body memories persisted with sadness, pain, and a conclusion was drawn by memories such as these, which affected my life forever more. I tapped on them all.

I tapped, *I can't play and be creative because I can't let my guard down – I must always be ready and alert to defend myself.* I wept as I tapped, *I'm not good enough to keep and she kept my sister so I must not be good enough.* I simultaneously fumed and mourned as I tapped, *the church they take me to won't protect me either.* I continued on tapping through the emotions, now raw and in full view, *so alone without family who love me and these adults frighten me!* My heavens, was I shocked when I found myself tapping, *I had to succeed financially or die and if they'll find out I'm a fake, it's better to be sick than to be dead.*

I tapped, *how could Jonathan treat me like this? Why didn't Jonathan defend me when malpractice occurred? Why didn't the doctor treat me before I stroked out? Why didn't the doctors admit they'd erred and help me recover?* After tapping for days, I was exhausted, but much had been revealed, and I was finished. I had directly faced my fears, anger and betrayals, as if looking into the dragon's face as it spit fire, burning my flesh. I stood my ground against my foe (my own subconscious), and surrounded (in my mind's eye) by legions of angels, I had survived. No, I now thrived, for what had been so fearsome when hidden in my bodymind, was now in the open. The ogres no longer had teeth to bite and marched my little piece of the Earth no more.

I was free of the feelings, both emotionally and physically. When I thought of the items on my list, I felt nothing. I remembered them all, but the memories no longer evoked an emotional charge. I could face the facts: I was rejected at birth, I was raised by violent sexual predators, I was a broken adult who did her best to survive, I was a victim of malpractice and my own husband didn't care enough to launch a defense for me, and I became a frightened dependant still striving to be kind to others.

Now I could return to the intellectual understanding that everyone in my life had done the best that they were able, and that they were all fallible humans just like me. I could forgive, in this sense. I would never need to do this again for my hurt and frightened feelings were neutralized. I no longer feared my subconscious, and the door to complete healing appeared to be just ahead on my journey to wholeness.

Soon after my Personal Peace Procedure marathon, a psychologist offered me a gratis session of Eye Movement Desensitizing and Reprocessing Therapy (EMDR). Within one hour of this work I clearly saw a false conclusion when under age five, that *if this how adults act then I don't want to be one.* It was then clear that this was one reason that the more successful I became as an adult, the more fearful I became. This EMDR session worked just like EFT had, in one sense: I faced a deeply buried feeling, came to terms with it, and it no longer had any emotional power over me.

I felt so blessed that I had been led to the point where I was fully receptive to both the outward signs and inner guidance that led me to these healing modalities. When thinking about the palpable spiritual protection I asked for and received as I faced my greatest fears, I was awed and amazed that I hadn't known to use them before. Most of all, I was moved to know that these healing practices and the loving beings surrounding me had brought about my sincere forgiveness of others, and the beginnings of self-forgiveness. When I was introduced to the book by Truman, I was not ready to face my feelings. Now I had faced them and felt the weight of a lifetime lifted away.

I realized that although I had been ready to do the work necessary to heal, my work was in fact limited to clearing away the resistance in both my conscious and subconscious mind to the all pervading love of Source. The total goodness---the perfection---could come into me only if I dropped all attachment to my ego. It was that self-definition of being an abused girl or willful woman or sad wife that had kept me apart, in my own sense of separateness, which prevented me from knowing that I was surrounded by the light. My ego was a wall of woundedness that kept me separate and in pain. When I was given the tools (because I had prayed for and accepted them), the wounded feelings of the ego could drop away. The little egoic "me" was not perfect, and would never be. But there is no "me" at all, in this respect: I can be filled with the perfection of God. I belong to Him and am made of Him. He, not little me, is perfect and finally able to manifest through me when I drop my ego. I take no credit then or now, for this is due to a clear "whoosh" of grace, in which we are only expected to do our part, which is to align our will with God's perfect will. I cannot even do my part without receiving a boost of strength from the Divine.

After this healing discovery, techniques for forgiveness appeared daily, allowing me to further transmute my pain into the flow of love.

As I had first done in my meditation room in Florida, I practiced guided meditations that led me into imaginary encounters with those I was now fully open to forgiving. With their pictures before me, I wrote letters to those I wished to forgive, and then ceremonially burned them, catching the wisps of ash in a bowl. Finally, I no longer felt the need to gaze into the eyes of those captured in print, contemplating both their lives and mine. I persisted in looking for the humanity, the frailty, and the imperfection in each of us, and I softened with the blossoming of compassion for us all.

Most of all, what I learned was that forgiveness was not for my tormentors' sake, it was for mine. The people I forgave were dead or forever missing from my life, but in this act, it opened a channel of reverence and compassion in me that was pure and without reservation.

Forgiving did not mean I condoned another's harmful acts, although I could now understand them and have compassion for my persecutors. In forgiving, I let go of the painful cords that had bound us together as perpetrator and victim. Perhaps in forgiveness, I thought, I was clearing the most injured part of my subconscious. With this, I imagined the cells of my body releasing their toxic burdens, restored to their inherent wellness.

It satisfied me to know that new healing tools would continue to appear when the time was right for me to use them. I do not believe that such appearances are coincidental, and if I try a healing practice and have marginal results, I know that if I remain receptive, it will bring me even closer to the tool that will cause total healing.

Now trusting that I was being led, no longer would I feel I had taken a wrong turn. My healing was imminent---I just knew it!

My library was growing with books that I excitedly looked forward to learning from. They seemingly were dropped off by invisible helpers. I cannot even explain how one book led to the next and the next, and a lecture or discussion led to still more. I was being readied for the next phase, the detoxification of both mind and body.

Detoxing the Bodymind

Later in 2010

I USED TO TRY TO CONTROL my outer circumstances through will, determination, bargaining and manipulating. Feeling alone and expecting the worst, I applied my logic and cunning to find methods leading to peace and joy. I had failed, to the point where my life was worse than was possible to imagine.

Now, through disciplining myself to focus upon new positive thoughts as I knew God or my Source wished me to, my life was changing for the better. Focusing upon the negative manifestations only perpetuated negativity, but I was less likely to revert to the negative since adding EFT to my toolbox. Transforming and spreading into even more unpleasant experience, I'd feel ever more buffeted about, and become even more lost in the quagmire of my own feelings and their outward appearances. Now, I was changing my life into what I had always desired, and my present moments were, in fact, better than ever.

With gratitude to our Source for revealing the truth to me, I no longer feared the power of the subconscious mind, and understood the way it had been programmed in my early life. I remained cautious about the behavioral tracks I imagined might remain, however. I knew that whatever had not been forever neutralized and replaced with a new positive approach, through tapping and meditation and grace, would continue to sabotage me.

> Prayer is the door to those great graces which our Lord bestowed upon me. If this door be shut, I do not see how He can bestow them. . . for His will is, that such a soul should be lonely and pure, with a great desire to receive His graces. (from The Life of Saint Teresa of Avila by Herself, translated from the Spanish by David Lewis)

Speaking of grace, I came to consciously understand this when I began praying to the Father. Still disconnected from the notion of a father doing anything good for me, I found that when I addressed this heavenly father with total surrender in my heart, admitting that I could do no better on my own, a whoosh of love and help was, without fail, forthcoming. I knew that there was certain work that no one but I could do, but that this consisted of continuous surrender and continuous willingness to focus my mind and apply my hands to the work before me.

It was no longer a given that I must press, unsuccessfully and repeatedly, against my prior programming. The automatic defaults built into my psyche, meant to protect me but instead harming me, had yielded through my efforts, and as I now realized, this was through grace. I saw and believed in the positive changes occurring physically, mentally, and spiritually. I had proof that the course of action I had been led to take after my direct connection experience was efficacious and a gift of our loving creator.

EFT was now a component of my daily life. I tapped on absolutely anything, mental or physical or spiritual, that disturbed me. Because of this daily clearing of emotions, I became more current with myself. By this I mean that I remained aware of what I was feeling, rather than compartmentalizing the feeling into my body, and then ignoring it. Journaling helps, and speaking openly of my conflicts and confusion to God the Father helps, but EFT has a way of quickly re-aligning me into a more peaceful state. Perhaps it can work for you, too, in this manner.

And may I speak of the importance of self-love? Realizing that to do otherwise was not kind to me, the beginnings of self-love and self-respect stirred within me. As I cared for my inner child, like the mother I had never had, I became ready to forgive myself for missing the mark.

Yes, I had approached life completely wrong, when I drew the childish conclusion that I must seize Earthly love and Earthly security in every way possible, feeling that it would never come to me naturally. I knew no better. Now I knew, and it was not too late to change.

I understood, at least intellectually, that I was worthy of love, both from myself and from others, for I certainly was worthy in my Father's eyes. But how was I to remove my own shame and dislike and self denial? With my new tool of tapping, of course, as I continued to pray.

I tapped to cancel my anger toward myself for all the erroneous decisions and actions I'd taken in life. This programming went deeply into me, for I had learned early on that it was safer to be perfect. I was flawed, but like others I had forgiven, I knew that I had done the best that I was able with the information I had. There was no shame in this. I did not deserve the punishment I had been giving myself, for not being a good enough person.

As I released my old patterns through tapping, and asked in prayer to be filled by the Shekinah, or the Divine Mother, I found that She was there all along. I did not need to be filled, for I had never been devoid of this either! I had only been unaware, except during the period of Samadhi following the NDE, or the blissful periods of my meditations of late.

I realized, in a blinding flash of insight, that since Source contains ALL and IS ALL, it contains all the qualities of mother, father, brother, sister, and friend. It contains, as I already knew, the angels and guides whose unseen help had led me to the point where I could call upon the Divine Mother or Father, directly. I realized that I was free to call upon whatever aspects of this WHOLE that I most needed in the moment.

Now my will was in alignment with the truth: My goodness, this was the correct use of my will! When I prayed, "Thy Will Be Done," this meant I was to ask that I come into alignment with ALL THAT IS. Goodness Itself, in other words. Although I lacked understanding when I prayed this in the past, I'd actually been asking to be one with the One all along! You probably also know that we learn through repetition, and each time I examined this concept of "God's will," I went deeper into true understanding of this.

I was journaling daily, and now used this tool not only to record, but to encourage new positive creations. If I could use it to describe what was happening, couldn't I also use it to describe what I wanted to happen? What a lovely lesson this was! I wrote long reveries of what my life was like if only in my dreams. How enjoyable it was to write, and later, to repeatedly read!

My nighttime dreams had eased. I used to dream almost every night of being pursued by a man with a knife. He was so clever that no matter how well I hid myself, I got stabbed. In such dreams, I felt myself dying, but the dream would end before my final breath. My other nighttime dream was of relieving myself in a bathroom that had no walls, in a stream that was endless, unable to hide myself from the other characters in the dream. In dreamland, I was either frightened by my pursuer, or humiliated during my most private moments. Now such dreams were rare.

I continued what was the seminal cause for all positive change that had occurred for me: I still meditated for at least an hour every morning and evening, and the peace from this continued to nourish me. I was one with the One, just God and me, particularly in those precious moments. How awesome this was, and what gratitude I felt, even though detoxifying my bodymind was an ordeal that I hoped would soon end. I was never alone through this, for my etheric friend from another life, the magical Mr. M, always appeared to meditate with me, and he encouraged me as the most loving of Earthly companions would have, throughout my days.

I also continued to be sheltered and embraced by what seemed to be legions of angels. I had the constant awareness that I was never alone, and that angels, unlike humans, were capable only of love. I knew that they were sheltering me through my days, and I ended every evening by calling upon Archangel Michael to protect me from all untoward energies that might be attracted to me, and to clear my path with his mighty sword so that I might reach full healing. I then called in Archangels Gabriel, Uriel, and Raphael, to guard the remaining four corners of my aura or energy body, and the Father and the Divine Mother (the Shekinah) to enclose me from above and below. In the safety of this cocoon of love, extended to us by Source Itself in its wisdom and compassion, I could sleep.

My learning came daily through such interactions with the Divine, but also from an increasing influx of information from my Earthly companions. I came to know so very many people dedicated to assisting others, through reading their books. An ever-growing library continued to fill me with new ideas to supplant the old and toxic ones regarding life.

I learned through the work of Lewis Mehl-Madrona ("Coyote Healing") and Alberto Villoldo ("Courageous Dreaming") that I fit the criteria of a fighter for whom a spontaneous remission from life-threatening disease is possible. The key components had appeared as a result of following Divine direction, to see myself, in my mind's eye, as well and whole.

As Dr. Mehl-Madrona points out, spontaneous remission is often accompanied by a "change of story," such as I had done. I was emboldened by Dr. Villoldo's words that "you have to reclaim your power to dream boldly and courageously, conscious of your journey through infinity. Only then can you easily and naturally let go of the fear that keeps you bogged down in your personal nightmares."

And so, I now had personal will to correctly exert, a growing knowledge base to apply, and ever stronger belief that I was going to survive and thrive. As Bruce Lipton put this in his preamble to "Spontaneous Evolution," we are "co-creators in the evolution of life. We have free will. And we have choices. Consequently our success is based on our choices, which are, in turn, totally dependent upon our awareness." I was choosing joyous life, trusting in Divine direction to make me whole, and now found this much easier to do than before.

I was absolutely amazed and thrilled to study Dr. Bruce Lipton's explanations, as a cell biologist, about the "Biology of Belief." From his perspective, everything I had learned from Alice Miller and Sue Gebhardt was scientifically true. I had been programmed as a small child by circumstances I likely would never fully remember. My environment had been toxic and had imbued me with this toxicity, through association.

Not only had my personal belief system been programmed regarding who I thought I was, I had been programmed about mankind's biological makeup. I had a cultural belief, as do most all of us, that dis-ease is the result of genetics, viruses and bacteria, and a large dose of bad luck. As I learned from Dr. Lipton, this is not true. Dis-ease results from environment, to include my mental and spiritual beliefs at the subconscious level, not only my physical environment.

The so-called acquired genetic mutation that my doctors cited as the cause of blood cancer was NOT the cause. The mutation was an effect, and I now knew how to change things at the level of cause (i.e. what I choose to think and feel), and this was a reason for rejoicing. My first cause became a strong belief that change for the better was inevitable as long as I kept my focus where I intended it to be, not allowing the distraction of appearances to the contrary.

I had my understanding of the act of creation further enforced by other books by Gregg Braden and Lynne McTaggart. I understood that supplication alone to a heavenly Father would never have worked for me, regardless of my feelings about fathers.

Effective prayer (as opposed to talking to God) is like visualizations, in that one must hold the belief that the work is already done, and celebrate that as fact rather than a hope or desire. This is true even with grace, for I *know* that it rushes in when I surrender, and I count on it just as I do with visualization. I am grateful, and am celebrating the miracle of grace, even before it whooshes in! This is what the Holy Ones had always been saying, but I had missed their point.

Humanity is interlinked, everyone is linked to All That Is, and change occurs at the macro level of mankind and our Earth, just as it occurs at the micro level within me. All creation is based on thoughts soaring into being through the feelings that give them strength. Supplication reinforces the notion that one doesn't have something and must *beg*. Supplication alone perpetuates the condition of lack, for it says "I need you to change what is." It says, "I don't have this." It is only when one asks, and believes that the desired effect is already granted and about to appear, that a supplication might work. But when one is in a dark tunnel and knows not what to ask for, grace will nonetheless rush in. When one has no more strength, strength flows in through grace. I may not ever understand the mystery of this, but it is so.

Thanks to all the knowledge, given through meditation and my teachers on Earth and in the heavens, I had already seen much manifesting for good. My reality had changed. As I changed my thoughts and feelings via visualization and affirmation and through humble talking with God (which in Jewish practice is called "hisbodidus"), my body changed. But there was more to do regarding my physical healing, as I learned. There is a delicate interplay between the body and its physical environment, and I was about to receive an advanced course on how to protect the body from the little spoken of, but very real physical dangers of life in this modern world.

I learned about this through talking with the next alternative medical provider I felt led to see. Another chiropractor, he introduced me to muscle testing, also called applied kinesiology, as a means to speak with my bodymind.

Sorry I didn't define this term before. . . what is bodymind? Ken Dychtwald may have been the first to use the term in his 1977 book, "Bodymind." It has come to mean that inter-related amalgam of both the physical body and the subconscious mind. Some have said, since his book came out, that the body IS the subconscious, for it embodies the feelings held at that level. The body also embodies conscious feeling, one must admit, however. Who has not felt embarrassment, and with that feeling perhaps blushed or began to perspire? There is another concept for which the bodymind is foundational, and this is the mind-body-spirit connection of which many have written. The M-B-S connection acknowledges the additional involvement at the level of Higher Self, Super consciousness, or one's spirit.

And now, back to the chiropractor who introduced this concept to me. . . Dr. G said that applied kinesiology would be an introduction to the *voice* of my body's own energy field. This procedure involved observing my arm muscle's ability to hold its strength, or not, when it was tested while holding a certain food or environmental substance.

Through muscle testing, we identified foods that were tearing down my health. My liver and kidneys, as hard as they had worked through all my years of illness, couldn't clear these toxins. I began weekly testing to adjust my diet and the supplementation program after going on a fast that I thought I might not survive! I was toxic not only because of the non-organic foods that had been a part of my diet, with the associated herbicides and pesticides used in conventional farming today; I was also very reactive to the chlorine and fluoride in my home's water supply. I switched to mountain spring water for drinking and cooking. I added a chlorine filter to my shower head. I avoided the swimming pool. I searched out a local supply of organic, non-GMO foods.

Not only what I took into my body, but what I put on my body, was important. I'd been unaware of the poisons in my body lotions, my perfume, and my cosmetics. I used the Environmental Working Group website for guidance on safer products, or made them myself so I knew what they contained.

I learned a great deal from the articles archived on Dr. Joe Mercola's eponymous website, and from Sayer Ji's site, "Greenmedinfo." When I subscribed to both daily newsletters, I became up to date on the latest holistic and natural alternatives to allopathic medicine. Reading about the toxicity and side effects of the prescription medications Jonathan and I were on, I made further changes. I substituted herbs and food substances for more of my medications with surprising success. I also added CoQ10 to Jonathan's pillbox to counteract the effects of the statins he took, and his anger level subsided a bit.

On a visit to Dr. G, I made a discovery: If I had eaten eggs over the past week, muscle testing revealed a new allergy to eggs. If I stopped eating eggs because of this, and switched to oatmeal, I would suddenly become allergic to oatmeal!

Being in an endless loop I imagined would culminate in not being able to eat anything whatever, I searched for more information, and by chance (wink-wink, you know now what a synchronicity looks like) I came across a book by Dr. Natasha Campbell-McBride describing her GAPS protocol. I began it right away, to heal from what I learned was leakage of undigested food through cell-sized openings from gut to body cavities and blood. This leakage caused my body to react as if these were allergens. This is called "leaky gut," and is quite common today due to our tainted food supply causing intestinal damage.

GAPS was the right method for me, for about three years. Through it, I eliminated sugar and grains, and increased my fat intake. The diet created a healthy state of ketosis that brought multiple benefits.

Although I eventually moved on from GAPS, I found that I couldn't re-introduce wheat or sugar, and all other non-gluten grains needed to be pre-soaked for twenty-four hours before preparing food using them. I still eat organic foods; I buy grass-fed beef direct from a local rancher, and poultry from a rancher who lets his fowl scratch in the dirt of his acreage for their food. I filter my drinking and cooking water through a Big Berkey. I take supplements to support my unique deficiencies, using a nutritionist plus my own research to determine what my body is calling for. I take herbs, rather than medications, for although their action might be slower than a prescription medication, healing from Mother Nature brings little to no side effects.

I've continued to learn and experiment since my GAPS experience. Based on the varied reactions of individuals to foods based on their tolerance for certain lectins (Dr. Peter D'Adamo, "The Blood Type Diet") and what we know about the variety of genetic predispositions (through analysis of your own genome through 23andme and others), we know that no two people will respond equally to the same diet and physical environment.

I also learned about the effect of electromagnetic frequencies (EMFs) on the body. A very timely and informative book on this subject is "The Invisible Rainbow: A History of Electricity and Life," by Arthur Firstenberg. If the body is an electrical field, then certainly the electrical fields around us are interacting with us energetically. I've taken measures to reduce the effect of EMFs within my home and am prudent in my cell phone use. I sleep on a grounding sheet, and have a grounding pad under my bare feet, as I sit in my office.

It is understandable that everyone will need to listen to their own body, and intuitively meet its requirements, in order to thrive. And in this effort, we support healing on the physical level, while the mind and the spirit continue to do their work.

While all the detoxing of mind and body progressed, my visualizations remained in conflict with what appeared to be true in the "real world" of manifestation. I imagined the feelings I would have as a totally well person as if true in the moment. But what was I to do when my doctors and my lab reports still said differently?

I continued in this belief that I was well, and I was no longer creating blood cell fragments and abnormally shaped and sized cells. My monthly blood test results looked quite normal, although I remained on a small dosage of interferon and could not be sure that I would remain normal if this was discontinued. Nonetheless, I imagined myself well, believing that more proof would follow. I continued to hear an inner voice saying, "Okay, the blood tests look perfect, they will remain so when you stop interferon, and you'll get a bone marrow biopsy proving that all the disease is gone." And so with strength I'm sure is grace I persisted in the prayer closet. I dwelt in the promise from 1 Corinthians 3:16: "Don't you know that you yourselves are God's temple, and that God's spirit lives in you?"

The Disease Disappears

February, 2012

IN THIS PHASE OF MY SPIRITUAL development, I easily cultivated compassion for others, and for the first time, myself. I found that my heart was an endless fount of love for mankind, my friends, and Jonathan. I prayed for them, always seeing their highest good coming to them, and realizing they were all loved and were never alone. I prayed for myself, too, with less guilt and more enthusiasm, for I understood that I was also a loved child of God, a unique creation of our Source. The simple instruction of Jesus to love the Lord your God, and to love others as yourself was becoming possible. How can one truly love oneself, unless you know yourself and then forgive yourself? Because of the steps I'd been led to prior to this, I was now capable of keeping this greatest commandment.

I no longer put others' needs before mine out of fear or lack of self worth. I served selflessly when needed, but took time to meet my own needs, in the little time permitted as Jonathan's care giver. I penciled in one or two hour periods for rest and nourishment of my body, my mind, and my soul. I called out to the heavens to restore me completely in those few moments. I arose at a very early hour in order to meditate, pray, and journal before getting Jonathan up at 7:30 AM.

Thinking of the love pouring into me, and knowing something or someone in the invisible intended me to be in a fellowship of love with others, I indulged myself in a few ways. I went away from our home once a week to attend an Edgar Cayce Study Group. This took care of my need for fellowship and independence. A monthly massage would have to take care of my need for relaxation and touch.

I had self love, but was not selfish. Through meditation, I was detaching from self obsession, and it was not the little me, but the Higher Self within me, that loved all God's creatures. That included me. I truly don't know why I never knew this before---I suppose that I was incapable before the transformative healing offered to me when I surrendered.

As a person who had once derived my worth from my career and possessions, and from others' opinions of me, I was now free to be loved and love myself for who I truly was. Yes, a work in progress, but worthy as are we all.

The Holy Spirit had a personality on occasion and clearly adored me. She had a sense of humor and took delight as I dwelled in Her teachings. Some walk with Jesus or Mother Mary, Krishna or Saraswati, depending on the religious orientation of the person experiencing this. For me, as you know, these personifications include guides, angels, and other spiritual beings, but also a sense that there is a Divine Mother within the greater Godhead from which we were conceived with that male, or Divine Father aspect.

186

It does not seem in vogue in the 21st century to believe in angels, but in prior eons when the Divine Feminine was preeminent, this was not questioned. The Bible and other holy works are replete with descriptions of angels, however. Inner teachers? This might be even more in question for some. But bear in mind that there are great religions such as Sufism and Hinduism in which the guru is foundational. The guru, also thought of as a teacher or a gateway to Source, will guide his disciples through demonstration but also through silent transmission. The guru may or may not be physically present when this occurs. The guru may have already made his transition to the other side, in fact. Isn't this what Jesus had become to me?

At this point in my development, it was exhilarating to have such rich interactions with the other side. Through silent knowing, and by seeing evidence of my protectors and friends through synchronicities, I knew that I would always receive answers when I sincerely asked and then trusted in this. Meanwhile, I had the companionship and love of wise teachers and friends. This phenomenon continues to enrich my life even today. I am intimately supported although my path has never been to work directly with physical teachers---my teacher has been "just" God in so many different aspects of the Godhead and Absolute, as I listen and follow direction through meditation and synchronicities.

There was much going on for me in inner space thanks to such loving interactions, and much to attend to in the physical world, too. Caring for my debilitated husband took almost all I had. Although stretched beyond my capabilities, this is what I had returned for: I left Heaven and learned to live in a broken body, to fulfill my desire to serve.

It seemed to me that Jonathan had dementia, as he was often disoriented, not remembering what we had just done or were about

187

to do. He never agreed to tests to confirm or deny his condition, but when his memory slipped he was defensive, abusive, and angry, and it always seemed to be my fault, no matter what had upset him. It was not just a contrary personality trait, as I had often experienced in earlier years with Jonathan, but something more extreme and unconscious.

A journal entry from this period describes the toss and turn of this:

When he arises, he complains of the smell of food in the condo. When the slightest extra movement is required of him he curses Jesus Christ. He interrupts my every phone conversation with commands and cursing, and afterwards demands lengthy explanations of what transpired on the call, as in his paranoia he has misinterpreted what was actually occurring. He complains of chocolate cake – now he wants something else like cheesecake. He points out that the cats have made nose prints on the window and looks to me to clean this immediately – if I do not then I am a slovenly wife. I leave the condo for a relaxing massage and a pleasant browse through a needlework shop, and when I return in an hour and a half he is frantically demanding that in the future I call him on the cell phone if I will be gone longer than this because the phone has rung twice and he doesn't know what to do. I hug him and tell him that everything is just fine, but his demeanor does not change for half an hour. When his blustering has ended, it is as though whatever it was that had disturbed him had never even occurred. He seems not to have even remembered it. He does not acknowledge that it happened. There is no apology, of course. And I treat him carefully so as not to experience a reoccurrence.

Through the years of our marriage, I became ill in my eighth year of it, and he became ill in our tenth year. I was getting better now, but he was getting worse. We had never been well equipped for emotional intimacy, and our communication skills weren't the best. We were celibate by our eleventh year together. The decades to follow had difficult periods, relieved by briefer periods of felicity. In spite of it all, we remained together and although our caring for each other was not perfect, caring was still a component of the relationship. There was loyalty; there was a basic need for companionship and to share our burdens together rather than alone (unless it was my illness). We had financial stability together, which we could not have had apart, and sometimes this was the only bond that, stretched almost to breaking like a rotting old rubber band, kept us united.

Acknowledging that the relationship was what it was, I continued in my resolve to be compassionate and kind, even if I did not receive this in return, and to continue to focus upon ways I could be a channel for love. This wasn't just sentiment or emotion. It was based on the knowledge that love is the greatest of all laws, and that it would burn up my own deficiencies while it blessed others.

And what was my relationship with Jonathan? Beginning as husband and wife almost three decades earlier, it had changed into a brother and sister relationship with the onset of our illnesses. Now, with his decline into dementia, it had changed to mother and son.

Strangely, to Jonathan, my easy chair in the den became very important. This was because I always meditated in this chair, and the energies had built up to extraordinary spiritual comfort. I loved myself, and felt the love of our Source, in this chair. No matter what went on in our home, no matter how troubling or fractious, I could retreat to this chair and be restored. Then I could arise again to surmount my own challenges and care for Jonathan. He was dependent upon me for most every mental, emotional, and physical need. I was responsible for his continued existence. If I could remain cheerful and optimistic, it was often the case that he would pick this attitude up from me and the "good periods" could be extended between the inevitable next inner storm and the next.

I knew through personal experience that union with the Holy Spirit leads to joy, to love, to peace, to strength, to firm inner knowing, to all good things. It is intimate and satisfying. I needed constant replenishment of this, and my chair in the den seemed to be the express lane to find relief again. Of myself, I was nothing, and it seemed that an accrual of this knowledge was stored in that well-worn chair.

Jesus taught that he and the Father were one, but he did no good works on his own. He said "The one who sent me is with me; he has not left me alone, for I always do what pleases him." (John 8:29) When we surrender to this, as he did, we can also say "I and the Father are one." (John 10:30) It is through surrender to this influx of love, while obeying the Holy Spirit's wisdom, that we only appear to do the work. It wasn't little me. As Jesus pointed out, "If I glorify myself, my glory means nothing. My Father, whom you claim as your God, is the one who glorifies me." (John 8:54)

I had grown beyond the hurts I had experienced with Jonathan. I had forgiven him although he had never asked for this, and I sought to give rather than to be given to. It was now an act of self love to offer unconditional love to him. The well from which I was drawing these feelings of love was deep, and I benefited from its flow through me to Jonathan. He did not know what he was doing, so how could I be offended by him? He needed my care and attention, and it was time to give up whatever was necessary.

I never gave up meditation or walking, however, and fit this in when he slept. As I walked the footpaths near my home, and in cadence with my foot falls, I affirmed *I am safe, All of my needs are being met. I am vibrantly healthy. Divine love is flowing in and through me and out to the world.* Every day, this affirmation rang out from my heart, and I both saw and felt each word. With every repetition, my feelings grew stronger. I broke into a wide smile, and tingled all over, as I experienced the bliss of being safe, loved, and healthy. Joyously, I sent these feelings out to everyone and everything.

Something shifted within me, and I realized that these affirmations were TRUE. They described my life as it really was. They were no longer the contrived wishes that I turned into desires that I turned into visualizations, but they were real in the present moment.

> Count on me in every act and stay among My own. In devoted service, keep your mind on Me alone. Think of Me and I shall clear your obstacles away; Acting out of ego, you shall never find your way. (from the 18th chapter of "Bhagavad Gita: The Song Divine" translated by Carl E. Woodham)

It was at this point that my monthly blood tests no longer required manual counts to identify aberrant cells! All of my counts were close to normal range as well. I had been visualizing for a few years that there would be a gradual shift into normalcy, and this was happening. My medication dosages reduced accordingly.

I knew that the wonderful blood count results I had been receiving for at least a year were proof of the physical healing. The results would continue to be good. I was absolutely sure of this. My heart burst with elation and gratitude. I was certain that when I received my next bone marrow biopsy, it would be perfect. Then there would be no question, even in the mind of my hematologist. I WAS WELL.

My next bone marrow biopsy would be my last, for this reason. Since the onset of the blood cancer about sixteen years prior, this was an annual event. Never pleasant, I dreaded them. I recalled the year a hemorrhage occurred on one side and the biopsy had to be repeated on the other. My return home was delayed because the clots might break free during a plane flight. Another year, I received a biopsy from a professional opera singer who sang in her huge voice as she pierced my hip, thinking it would distract me from the pain of having this done without anesthesia. It did not.

There was also the emotional imprint of the biopsy at my Sarasota doctor's office, complete with Jonathan's upbraiding of me, and my vomiting out of the opened car door as we drove home.

I knew this time would be different.

My last biopsy revealed that I was at least half way into the final phase of MF. Yet my blood test results were so utterly normal now, that I believed that my bone marrow would also look this way. Now, as I walked, I visualized even more:

I see my doctor sitting across from me in the exam room. He is looking at the bone marrow biopsy report for the test just performed. He says to me, "It is perfect. I can't explain it, but you are totally well!"

I visualized just this for the three months leading up to the next biopsy, seeing this in my mind's eye as I walked the nature trail. I saw myself being positioned in the procedure room, slipping my ear buds on so I would hear Mozart instead of the patter of my attendants while I was under anesthesia. I also saw myself asking them not to say anything negative even if what they saw disturbed them. I always ended this visualization by fast-forwarding to the doctor's exam room, hearing his words of amazement when he reviewed the results.

Finally, the day arrived, and everything went just as I had envisioned it would. I saw the attendants drawing perfect bone marrow as I floated in a Mozart reverie. A few weeks later, I was ushered down a hall to my exam room, fairly bursting with anticipation. A knock at the door, and I was joined by my doctor.

"Well, let's see what the results are," he said as he signed into the computer on the desk before him. Looking dignified in a dark business suit, with his tie slightly loosened, he leaned forward to better see the screen. Everything seemed to move in slow motion. "Well, my goodness, there is no collagen fiber and the reticulin fiber is gone! Really? Let's look again," he said with surprise.

"My goodness, the results are perfect!" he exclaimed, as our eyes locked.

I replied, after I let the import of his words sink in, "I'm not surprised. I knew that I've been well for some time, now."

With this, we both arose, and hugged. Then he opened the door, and leaving it ajar, walked down the hall to his staff office, where I could hear him exclaim, "She was in a wheelchair! I cannot explain it, but she's totally well!"

When he returned to the exam room, his face flushed with emotion, we again hugged, and I said, "I cannot thank you enough for everything you have done. You did everything that medical science knew to do, and you did it with great kindness. I am grateful, but I want you to know that I did some things, too."

With that, I told him about the visualizations I had been practicing. I told him about the detoxing of my mind and my body, and the connection I once again had with our Source, and how blessed I knew myself to be.

He said, "I have no doubt that all of your efforts made a difference. Regardless, this is amazing. Congratulations!" and we parted, with feet barely touching the floor.

This event was over nine years ago, at the time of this writing. Ever since that day, I have felt several distinctions must be made about what occurred. First, my healing was not sudden, as is often described in literature about so-called spontaneous remissions. It took about two years to see proof of my healing in blood test results, and I was at the four year mark when the bone marrow biopsy which had for the first time been delayed almost a year beyond normal, that we had the final confirmation that the disease was gone. I view this healing as incremental, rather than sudden, for these reasons. Second, it was not a remission. It was a cure, per the medical definition of it, given the amount of time I have been cancer free. It was not, however, a miraculous cure. This was no miracle. It was simply an application of the understanding of divine law, as I learned it through my meditations, through study, and through endless experimentation. How did I come to know the law, and to discipline myself to surrender unceasingly to it? Now, that may have been a miracle, after all!

I now knew through experience that Divine Wisdom has a soft voice of authority. It is a calm and constant frequency---all we ever do is hush the noise of daily life that keeps us from hearing it. It does not lie. It cannot. You will know it when you hear it. If you do not apply the lesson it teaches in that moment, you will not receive further lessons. It is patient. It will wait for you to learn, and then you will be taught the next step for your spiritual growth.

For any appearance of lack, if we ask in prayer believing (my form of prayer being a seeing and believing that all will be perfected), you will receive assurances (as I did) that it is God's good pleasure to give you the Kingdom. The Kingdom encompasses all that is good---not just the good health that I now speak of.

When we contact Spirit in the silence of our mind that Spirit will teach us in ways that correct our thinking, feeling, speaking, and acting. And we are swept up in God's love. And we feel His sense of humor and tolerance of our foolish ways.

Wisdom offers to be your daily guide and protector. It expresses through intuition, through perhaps an inner voice, or through obvious synchronicities or signs. It leads always to greater understandings, improved practices, and a never-ending quest for more closeness, and more responsiveness to its whisperings.

I was blessed to have been pushed to the point in life where I was open to learning such things. It was through my agreement that I would suffer in order to grow that I had reached this moment. Remember that mystical moment in my bathroom while preparing to go to work, when I had an encounter with an unknown part of myself and made an agreement with it? This is what I had agreed to do: Years of suffering bringing knowledge and then my release into wholeness.

> Citing the Vedanta, I shall now explain to you five considerations that influence what you do: One who acts, the body, all the senses, and the deed and, of course, the Supersoul, determine what succeeds. Right or wrong, all that you do with body, words, or mind comes about because of these five factors I've defined. One who disregards these five and thinks himself in charge lacks the good intelligence to see things as they are. (from the 18th chapter of the "Bagavad Gita: The Song Divine" translated b Carl E. Woodham)

Some years after the disappearance of the disease that was to have killed me, a book called "Radical Remission: Surviving Cancer Against All Odds," written by Kelly A. Turner, Ph.D. was released. In it, Dr. Turner describes the nine key factors for "radical remission." They are as follows:

- Radically change your diet

- Take control of your health
- Follow your intuition
- Use herbs and supplements
- Release suppressed emotions
- Increase positive emotions
- Embrace social support
- Deepen your spiritual connection
- Have strong reasons for living

I was stunned when I read Dr. Turner's book, for she had identified each of the components of my own healing. The only caveat I would make is this: My social support was from the other side, not from Earth, yet it was so strong and dependable that it was as powerful as any help that might have come from an Earthly network of supporters.

Life As It Should Be

2012-2014

IT HAPPENED JUST AS I IMAGINED it, only better. The doctor, after uttering the words I had heard with my inner ears for months, arose from his chair and fairly ran out into the hallway leaving the exam room door open, and I heard him say, "She was in a wheelchair and now she is well!"

After this, I drove home in a state of gratitude and awe. All credit belongs to our amazing Creator, our loving Source. It had led me in baby steps to this healing. This was the stupendous ending of years of lessons, and unending encouragement to move beyond my failures until I had enough experience and confidence in the law of love to yield to this measurable effect. What we ask for, we are given by the Source of all good things, although it can come only as quickly as we can accept it.

How could I explain this outcome to others? The need to share what I experienced, whether it was the life-changing knowledge given while on the other side, the desire to help those who were suffering or about to die alone, or now this firsthand demonstration of the law that we create our reality through our thoughts and feelings instead of the reverse, as I had thought during my life before I sought God above all else. . . there was so much I felt compelled to share with others and I did not know how but knew that I would work through it with the guidance of my loving Higher Self. The answers, and the will, and the appropriate thoughts and feelings would come. The first step was to believe that it would happen in the perfect way at the perfect time.

I realized as I drove home that Jonathan would not be able to share in my joy. He would not understand. Jonathan was unreceptive to anything that deviated from what he had been taught worked, such as a prescription for an infection. He viewed it like this: There are medical experts who know what the best methods are, and you disobey at your own peril. There was no such thing as a healing by God, for there was no God. I once felt that way, too, and understood his reluctance to let go of what appeared to be his own best hope. From his perspective, what I'd experienced was beyond conventional reasoning, so, it surely had a logical explanation other than the only one I could offer.

I longed to make a heart-to-heart connection with Jonathan, and to convince him to lean less on pharmaceuticals and more upon changing his thoughts and feelings. But what was more charitable? To treat him as I would want to be treated, or to treat him as he would want to be treated? To say his dependence and trust in his doctors wasn't enough, and that he should see himself well, instead, would be taken like an insensitive criticism. Hadn't I once reacted with anger when a well-meaning friend gave me Louise Hay's book, "You Can Heal Your Life"? I wasn't open to the concept yet, and took offense. I would not tell Jonathan that his thinking was the root cause of his current malaise when he was already so far gone that he could barely cognize sufficiently to eat and bathe. It was too late for the effort of learning to control his mind and emotions, and it was unlikely that he would have responded to my offer to help him understand, even if it was not at this late stage of his deterioration.

And so, although I told Jonathan that the bone marrow biopsy showed that I was miraculously disease-free, it was so inconsequential to him that he soon forgot it. He continued to think I still had MF although I was completely free of it.

My doctor's plan was to keep me on a small dosage of interferon as a precaution since he knew of no other case like mine. I was adamant about quitting, and after debate, followed by outright rebellion, I stopped of my own volition.

As I look back on this period, there are certain things I did that stand out. To summarize them all in a single phrase: I died to self daily. St. Paul describes this intentional act, and make no mistake that only saints can get away with doing this only once daily. For me, it had to be hourly and even by the minute.

In the particulars, there were certain practices that emerged as I listened to my Higher Self's teachings while in meditation, and responded to the synchronistic events presented by the angelic beings, my primary companion (the magical Mr. M), and the angelic experts and master teachers that came and went as needed. These practices are still my way of life. I shall not say that they are the ideal practices for you. You are unique and will find your own. With the following, I remained stable through years of additional care giving to Jonathan, and beyond that to a new life you'll soon learn about as you continue reading. Here are some of the things I do:

- I acknowledge my empathic nature, and through a close examination of myself I parse out "what feelings belong to me" and "what doesn't"

- I stay in the present by tapping, journaling, and feeling the feelings rather than storing them away in my bodymind
- I deliberately seek the "next better feeling," if I find that I'm not experiencing my highest level of love and joy. How? I ask myself: "Could I put a better spin on my current situation?" I keep asking this daily until I've spiraled up as far as I can go. (See the Abraham-Hicks books to learn more about the how and why of this.)
- Rather than controlling as I once did, I surrender and trust in the guidance, the wisdom, and lofty intentions of God. I stay meek and humble. I know in my heart that everything is always in perfect order as I take the steps presented to me to do.
- I savor both the obviously good, and the elements that seem bittersweet. Each moment taken this way is a beautiful and rich eternity. There is so much within a single moment it is almost more than I can take in.
- I pay attention to how my body, my mind, and my emotions are doing. I pay attention to my spiritual closeness, too. When I stumble, as do we all, I ask that Divine Love first fill me to overflowing, so that I can love others as they deserve. I'm flawed, and need to lean on grace after I've done all I know to do.
- I "meet people where they are" and do not feel it is up to me to change them. I want only to love them, unconditionally, just as I strive to do for myself. This is related to my personal take on the Golden Rule, which is, "Do unto others not as you would have them do unto you, but as they would have you do."
- I end my day with self-evaluation. Then, in my mind's eye, I revise what occurred into what my better self would have done instead, and ask that this be the memory recorded in my subconscious.

- I look for everything great and small that I can feel grateful for. This is especially nice to do when I arise in the morning.
- I meditate---I meditate---I meditate. There is nothing more to be said than this. All good comes from it.

Who knows what each new day will bring in the life of a sick patient and the care giver? It is always something, but if you truly love God, nothing will disturb you. Ask for help to do this, care giver or not! You will live in peace. You'll be detached and one with the One, just you and God. To know nothing but God is to know joy. The point of meditation and devotion is not to sit in meditation all day. The permanent and abiding awareness of being in the presence of God, made of God, for God---that is the point of living such a life. The contemplative state of detachment, of being in the "now" with no personal stake in the game, is the end result of a steady meditation practice.

Grateful for having personally moved from a broken state to one of wholeness, I felt *blessed* to remain a caring helpmate to my husband. Having forgiven him for all that he had done or might still do, I was fully present to Jonathan's physical needs and his fragile soul. This was what I'd come back from the other side to do: To serve what was, in hindsight, my greatest earthly teacher.

His pain was constant and severe. No matter the medication or the dosage, he never felt complete relief. He complained of this, and I understood. Yet once, I impulsively said to him, "Suck it up" when he said he couldn't stand the pain any longer. What a thoughtless thing this was, and yet my saying so led to a great healing. His face immediately registered his feelings. His eyes dropped with shame, and he said softly, "I'm so sorry I said that to you. I don't know how I ever could have. That's how I used to motivate my Special Ops guys! Now, I get it. Forgive me." How sad it was that he was in this condition now. I wept inside, not wanting to hurt him by shedding tears outwardly. His moments of clarity were few, and this moment had been pivotal for us both.

As he dwindled, my meditation practice sustained me but my studies necessarily diminished. My emotions now flowed in and out like the ocean. I didn't suppress my feelings as I would have in the past, nor did I dwell on them like I would have before. In the moment, my purpose was service. I clung to Source, I worked with every tool I knew to stay close to Source, and I surrendered to that great One in all things. The challenge was this: Could I see the joy in the midst of human frailty, both Jonathan's and mine? My focus was upon love of others, myself, and our ineffable Source. Yes, I felt sadness as I kept daily watch over Jonathan. At a deeper level, I understood that all things pass, and what was happening could not be resisted, but only supported. I listened closely for inner guidance, asked for wisdom, and for the willingness to obey when direction came.

Inner guidance had a word for me, and a word for Jonathan. For myself, I heard that "the Lord of Life is my shield and my shelter and in Him I trust." For Jonathan, I was to tell him this every day: "I love and accept you exactly as you are."

The final few years of care giving were the most challenging. I arose hours before dawn to shower, dress, and meditate before waking Jonathan. I balanced and bathed him, then slipped his arms into a tee shirt, and one leg at a time, guided him into shorts as he sat on the side of his bed. Then, I'd guide him to his easy chair, holding the oxygen cannula away from his body so we would not trip.

When our LPN, Cherie, would arrive to give me a few hours of respite, she'd listen to his stories of being a football hero, and chuckle with him over his high school antics. This distracted him from wound care and the daily ordeal of pulling compression stockings up his legs, to fight against swelling. He became a much softer and kinder person toward me, thanks to the buffer she provided during my little rest, and socializing with her brought out his more generous qualities.

For three years, he coped with the need for oxygen, accompanied by the constant thumps and wheezes of his concentrator, his world limited to the distance his cannula would stretch. The oxygen machine, along with a CPAP, was so noisy that I could no longer spend my nights in the same room with him. His restless leg syndrome cut and bruised my legs as he thrashed about in troubled sleep. Because we had only one bedroom, I bedded down on an inflatable mattress in the den, drawing shut the drapes that separated this room from the main living quarters. I slept fitfully like this for a year, before I reluctantly accepted that I could not continue.

I found a house nearby, with a bedroom at either end. Cherie transported Jonathan to our new home, empty except for an easy chair. She settled him there and entertained him until I arrived with the moving van. The movers assembled Jonathan's bed first, and as soon as it was up and ready, we moved him to his room where he slept through the noises of furniture and boxes being brought in.

Prior to move day, I'd invited friends to write positive affirmations and Bible quotes on the walls of every room. Then, all was painted over in soft whites and aqua. Because Jonathan was color blind, life appeared monotonously greenish gray to him, but these colors, which he had chosen, seemed vibrant to him. Little did he know that he was also being infused with the healing vibrations of the affirmations beneath the wall paint!

His trips away from home were a challenge. We'd sling a portable oxygen tank over his shoulders, painful due to torn rotator cuffs, and then switch him from concentrator to tank. He couldn't slide into the car without help, and would cling to a removable handle placed in the car door latch, while I helped him twist and lower himself. Then, he'd take the oxygen tank onto his lap.

Upon arrival, I'd lift his Big Man walker from the back of the SUV. Jonathan was a large man, even at this late stage. He was over 6'4" before his surgeries, but now he could look eye-to-eye with me, at my full height of 5'3". He never dropped below 303 pounds, in spite of having no taste for food. It was worth it to see his face light up when he sat on his walker, paused in an aisle at Costco, watching folks go by. This was a treat for him, compared to his weekly doctor appointments.

Interminably, this comprised the tedium of his life. One day, we were sitting in our kitchen nook, still dappled with morning sunlight. Something different had arisen. We seldom talked, but he wanted to tell me something. "Em, what is happening? A woman is coming to me in the night and asking me to take her hand and get up." I saw distress in his soft dark brown eyes. He had never known me for who I really was, but liked to think that perhaps I was a good witch. His definition of a good witch came straight from the Hallmark movies that delighted him when he watched these before bedtime. Good witches can be turned to, to interpret one's dreams, you see.

I didn't mind if he thought of me in this way although it was not true. Certainly, he'd had less than favorable thoughts of me before this, and I viewed this as a great improvement over the past. I replied to his question with another question. "Honey, can you tell me what she looked like? Her face? How she was dressed?"

"Well, she had a kind looking face. She didn't want to scare me. She was white. Her dress and her face and hands."

"Really? You mentioned her face. Could you see her entire body, honey?"

"No, just her arms and her face," he said. "I guess I didn't see her legs."

"You didn't recognize her, did you?"

"No," he said, "But she seemed friendly. Maybe I knew her, I don't know. She reached her hand toward me and asked me to come with her. She had her other hand on my chest. . . she was so gentle and sweet. Her hands were soft, like yours. I liked her. . . but don't get what's happening."

I felt a surge of love for him as I thought about how to answer him. I'd read books in preparation for what might now be happening. He was approaching the terminus, I thought, for he no longer did much but sleep during both the days and nights of his pared down life. He refused anything other than homemade coffee cake in the morning and a bagel in the afternoon. The freezer was chock full of his favorite ice cream for evenings, and I intended to never run out. His lifelong habit of making coffee persisted, but he drank no more than a few sips. I couldn't force him to drink water, or to eat more. Even his favorite dinner dishes now repulsed him, and turning his anger outward, he would accuse me of changing the recipe, or forgetting how to cook. How long could life be sustained like this, if he refused to eat?

What could I say to him, when I suspected that, like the hospice stories I'd read, he was now being helped by some kind force from the other side to let go? I knew that he was torn, as he felt that his life was now just a blur of drugs and sleep, punctuated by 3 AM insomnia. He sensed that it would get no better. Yet, he did not want to let go of his life, for he felt that there *was* no life after this Earthly existence. He didn't want to disappear into nothingness.

I thought, perhaps this is why this unknown helper has appeared! Perhaps he can, with a repetition of this nightly event, lose enough fear to let go. I knew from my own journey to the other side and back that our bodies cannot die until we will it to be so. How sad to be trapped in this failing body and mind, slipping in and out of the fog of dementia, pained by so many failing bones, muscles, and nerves, yet not know how to let go.

And so I said, "Sweetheart, I don't think this is a malevolent spirit coming to see you, but it *is* a spirit. . . so how would you feel about greeting her nicely if she visits you again?"

He was silent for a moment, and then replied, "I'll try. It's sort of comforting when I see her. . . it's just that it's so strange."

A few days later, he reported that she had visited again, and it still was disturbing. She had behaved just like prior visits, reaching to him and touching his chest, and he just wasn't sure that this was okay. "Is it the drugs?" he asked.

I replied, "It's possible," but whether or not it was the drugs, "It'll probably be easier if you try to relax and enjoy her visits though, don't you think?"

The next day, he said that he could not relax about this, at all. I decided that I would help him, as I had helped others in the past who were troubled when they came to me for psychic readings. I knew that it was helpful to them for me to use props. The positive mental image of my prop could be embraced by him as a positive sign for his future. Why not use props now to ease Jonathan's mind? Hoping it would help, I volunteered, "Sweetheart, you think this isn't a good spirit that has been visiting you, and I trust you. So I'm gonna do something to make sure she doesn't come back, if that's okay with you. All right?"

"*Yes*, do whatever you can!" He was sad and a bit frightened, and so I assured him that my actions would take care of this once and for all.

I promised, "You needn't worry about it again." I asked him to move to his easy chair so that he could watch what I was about to do. I said, "You know that I'm a bit of a witch. Well, sit back while I do my work."

I lit a fat cheroot of white sage, blew the leaf ends to a red glow, and began to waft the fragrant smoke into the northwest corner of the living room. With deliberation, I worked my way to each corner of the room as he watched, and assured him, "Only good can exist in this lovely smoke."

I would chase all the bad, if there was any, out of the house. I went room by room, working into corners, into closets, and around windows and doors. As I did so, I silently prayed for Jonathan's highest good, and for divine protection and love to shower down into our home to comfort him. After I finished the interior of the house, I offered more. "Jonathan, I'm going to go outside now. . . back soon, after I sprinkle salt at the four corners of the yard. I'm going to make an invisible fence to keep all the bad out. Then, no worries any more. You'll never again be disturbed, and you'll never have to wonder about the visitor's intentions. If she continues coming at night, you can trust that she's a good spirit, okay?"

He seemed relieved, and laying back into the recliner, he closed his eyes.

A few weeks later, still receiving occasional visits, but no longer disturbed by them, we had an interlude of lucid conversation. Sitting in the kitchen nook with morning light streaming in from the south-facing windows, he looked directly at me, and said, "I know you don't think that I love you, but I do." He said, "Remember when I was playing ball out of town, and I borrowed a buddy's cell phone to call you? I just wanted to hear my little Emily's voice and tell you about the game."

I said "Yes, I remember. . . that was a sweet moment. Thank you."

"Well," he continued, "I'm no good at telling you I love you, and I've treated you poorly sometimes, and really don't deserve you. You've been so good to me, and I just. . . I never deserved to be with such a good person as you." He went on, with the words, "I'm sorry I never treated you well enough, like you deserve to be treated. I don't deserve all the care you've given me. I've been a burden, and I'm sorry. You've been so kind to me, and I don't know why."

With tears welling up, I said, "You are more than welcome. I'm glad to have been here to help you, and I'm glad that I've been well enough to do what you've needed. You know, I love you, too." With this, I felt the years of sadness resolve into closure. I knew that although we were not perfect, we both had done the best we could with the capabilities we had, and there was love between us.

I found Jonathan on the floor, having passed away during the night, about three weeks after his assurances. He had returned to a state of dementia and drug-induced fog since those sweet words, but I saw no further physical declines, and did not realize that death was so very close.

The paramedics explained that judging from the position of his body on the floor, Jonathan had arisen from bed during the night, and a massive heart attack killed him before he hit the carpeted floor. I thought, with a sharp intake of my breath as shock punched into my belly, *did he take her hand?*

More than I Could Imagine

2014-2020
Within Arizona

YEARS HAVE PASSED SINCE THEN. After Jonathan's death I remained cancer free, but endocrine weaknesses gave way to chronic Epstein Barr and Cytomegalovirus. Selfless service was good for my soul, but had taxed my body. I didn't yield to the need for rest during his illnesses, or for months after his passing.

In spite of seventeen years of care giving that increased in intensity until Jonathan's abject dependence upon me, it was still a shock when he died. The tears flowed endlessly, chapping my face and reddening my swollen eyes. My life with Jonathan had lasted for thirty-four years. We shared in the changes that had rocked us from one coast to the other and back again. We had endured his surgeries and dementia as well as my death and return to my own damaged body and mind.

He had said when we were RVers that he would not live past seventy-two. This is what he wished for me to plan for as I calculated how I would make our nest egg last as long as we did. He died about two months before his seventy-second birthday, just as he said. Jonathan could have easily lived twenty more years in the horrible state of limbo he was in, had he not yielded to death this way.

He left, as I had prayed for so long that he might. He left without suffering, given that it was so quick he passed before his body fell to the floor. I used to imagine that I was speaking to his Higher Self, saying that it would be so good for Jonathan to go home and be healed, then come back in a fresh new body. But I knew I had nothing to do with it. We all have a free will choice about when we shall exit and only Jonathan's clear choice would have made this possible. I knew this, not from theology, but from my own experience with my own death and return.

It comforted me to think that in his final moment, he took the ethereal hand that had been offered to him and was accompanied by a loving companion to our Home. That woman. . . was she a mother figure of his own creation, or maybe an angel from his own legion of heavenly support?

My first morning without Jonathan, I saw that the salt lamp beside his easy chair was extinguished. Next, although it wasn't my habit to do so, I turned the stereo on. Soft jazz filled the inner spaces of my home, and I felt eased. Jonathan didn't care for jazz, but he knew that I did. Had he tuned to this before bed the night he passed? Did he know what was ahead? Had he thought of me?

That evening, I turned the cable TV on. The selection queued up for viewing was the movie called "An Unfinished Life." The next movie in Jonathan's watch list was "The Breaking Point." When wiping the table in the kitchen nook, I lifted Jonathan's stack of papers away, and two cards fell out. I'd given them to Jonathan more than a year prior. They spoke of my love and assured him I would never leave. He'd secretly kept them. What a wave of relief I felt as I recalled saying the same things to him less than a week prior. I'd told him that I loved him just as he was, he needn't struggle to change a thing, and that everything was fine between us.

Now alone, I sought a new normal. What did I know and love more than anything? What would restore me now? Meditation, of course.

I tried and failed to meditate that second evening alone. I could not, for when I closed my eyes, I had only a flashback of his body on the floor. The next morning, I was at odds. There was no longer a need to arise at 5 AM. My care giving function, my only function except to stay close to the All That Is, was gone. *What did I do before I was a care giver?* It had been so long, I could not remember.

If I couldn't center myself through meditation, I knew I could speak out loud, or in my heart, of my sorrow and need for help. I was unable to affirm a vision of peace and joy for myself, but I could fall upon grace in such a moment as this. I asked for contact with my guides and angels, and to know what to do in order to heal my heart. My body was sick from viruses and failed adrenals, but I was used to "playing hurt" so I didn't stop to rest.

Exploring for soft music to comfort me, I was led to a beautiful chant by Deva Premal which uses the timeless Sanskrit words of the Gyatri Manta. I did not know that I was listening to her interpretation of one of the most revered Hindu mantras of all time, but it soothed me as I played it many hours each day. It beckoned me to learn the words, and I painstakingly wrote them down phonetically, and began to chant with Deva. When I eventually looked for a translation I was not surprised to see that once again God had called me to seek solace in Her Beauty. One interpretation of this chant, in English, is as follows: "O Divine mother, our hearts are filled with darkness. Please make this darkness distant from us and promote illumination within us."

I also was led to a book by Father Thomas Keating, and being unable to practice meditation as he teaches (a technique called Centering Prayer) for I could not bear it, this led me to the comfort of praying the Rosary for the first time. I was greatly comforted by the rosaries written by Fr. Michael Adams, in his "Rosaries of Divine Union: Rosaries for the Contemplative Dimension of Prayer," which he kindly offers for free on the Internet. I was then blessed with a well-worn Franciscan rosary, given to me by a local Catholic parish, and I prayed the decades, chanting to the Divine Mother in this way until her gentle qualities revealed themselves to me.

Becoming accustomed to the movement of the beads under my fingers, and seeking a simpler way to give my mind up, I was led to do one word chants using a Rudraksha mala. Letting these round seeds pass slowly through my fingers, I inwardly intoned "Love" or "Elohim" over and over, lulling myself into stillness and peace.

My inner voice next led me to a local church. I came to know some congregants, volunteered to help with the Women's Auxiliary, and enjoyed many a metaphysical discussion with its minister, a former Russian Orthodox Bishop. He had no outlet for his mystical nature. I welcomed the teaching he passed on to me from his mentor, a fellow Bishop who'd endured twenty years of imprisonment in the Gulag Archipelago.

Why not start a meditation group? The students' energy will make your meditations easier. My guides suggested this, and Pastor S confirmed it. I set to work developing study materials, lesson plans, and procuring church space for the class. But before this launched, I was to have a rare privilege. Pastor S turned an entire Sunday over to me, to lead and to preach.

I gave a sermon describing my experience of the Holy Spirit which is within us all. The Holy Breath, the Ruach, the Comforter, was, as I see it, the reason for all the guides and angels helping me on my life's journey. I explained I'd resolved to know nothing but God, and this led to a so-called miracle that utterly changed my life.

There were tears in the eyes of the congregants as they lined up to embrace me after the service. Moved by what we'd shared, some asked to learn meditation with me.

My class filled with hungry students, and as my inner guides had promised, I felt the vibrations of my fellow devotees lifting me up. In their presence, I could slip into the comfort of meditation, no longer troubled by flashbacks of Jonathan's final moment. Time passed, the students learned, and we all reached a point of independence with the practice. All had worked for good. My inner voice and synchronicities then led to my next phase as a single woman.

It would be best to start anew, elsewhere. I'd leave the desert for the mountains, leave eternal summer for four seasons, and become a part of a small town where people walked their dogs and stopped to chat on the green grass of an abundance of downtown parks.

On my second house hunting trip, my agent said, "There's a home that just came onto the market this morning I think you should see. I know it isn't on your list, but we're close to it now." Within minutes, we were on the side of a mountain, and surrounded by Alligator Junipers and tall pine trees. We walked down flagstone steps to the front courtyard, jiggled the key free from the lockbox, and entered. I knew that I was home.

I'd prayed that the angels would guide me, and that circumstances would not push me past my physical endurance, meager due to the viruses. My prayers had been answered! I'd imagined a house in the woods, and here it was, at the end of a lightly paved road that followed the curve of a mountain slope in the midst of dark woods. It was meant to be. *This will be my life*, I thought. *I'll recover my health in the peace of the crisp air, here in the silence of the forest. I'll meditate and write and walk the trails. I'll go to bed, and I'll rise again, in tune with the sun.*

I spent the entire summer meditating and resting there. As I'd imagined, I'd sit on the balcony, taking in the air, as I looked upwards to watch hawks circle on the air currents above me. Then perhaps I'd call in the deer. Soon they would enter from a thicket of tasty bushes at the east side, coming in groups of four or five, with black and white tails tucked. They'd leave their hoof marks in the pea gravel trail made especially for them at the edge of the property. Sometimes, they would stop and look up at me with their deep brown eyes, and I'd send my love to them.

I did little else that summer besides nourish my body, mind and soul. Then a friend suggested I not give in to my notion to remain single. "Why not try an online dating service and meet people? You aren't meant to be alone," she said, over tea. After all, it had been about two years since I'd been widowed.

Not realizing I was creating a public posting at a dating service, I answered questions that I thought would lead to learning what dating services do. What a surprise when "Jonathan" wrote, saying that we had a lot in common and he would love to meet me. Still ambivalent about starting over, I decided that I would wait three months, and if he continued to write I would join the dating service so I could write back to him. But he wrote every few days. *What had I gotten into?* Decades of a marriage that had rendered me an innocent in the new world of online dating, and feeling vulnerable, I persisted in my plan to wait.

The next time I meditated I received authoritative direction: "Grab your credit card and enroll when this is over. You must meet him." By now, having learned to listen to my inner voice, I wouldn't ignore what my logical mind thought was bad advice. I was living in the moment, and trusting that I was being led for my highest good. I knew that there was no such thing as a coincidence, and that everything happening in the movement of my eternal life was leading me, teaching me, and blessing me. I knew that there was no such thing as a mistake. There could only be delays in the inevitable goodness that would manifest for me.

Knowing all of this, I followed my orders, and within a day, Jonathan and I were in touch by phone. *What a bad joke on the part of the Universe to bring another man into my life when I was all done with men. In particular, did it have to be another man named Jonathan?* If we saw each other enough that I need speak of my late husband, would he think I was trying to resurrect the former Jonathan through him?

With pepper spray at the ready, I met him for the first time. What did I know? Prepared to be uncomfortable, and ready to flee the coffee house, this man instead intrigued me. In our first words, precious information came forth: He had taken spiritual vows while in his twenties, and had lived first in a Buddhist monastery, and then worked and lived at a Self Realization Fellowship retreat center for several years. He'd come to the area to learn from another holy person, a Tibetan Rinpoche, who lived in the nearby hills. He, like me, was a constant seeker of truth and closeness to the One, and knew that the One can appear in many guises but in every instance is boundless love. Jonathan was an artist, a musician and singer, an inventor and entrepreneur. He was creative, independent, and deeply spiritual.

He seemed cautious as he disclosed he'd lived a life of meditation, and listening to his inner voice had led him to paths seldom traveled. He'd lived a life in which spiritual retreat and secular life had been interleaved. He'd been blessed to be in long companionship with not one, but two of Paramahansa Yogananda's direct disciples, living in community with them for long stretches of time. Their years as guru and a direct channel of spiritual energy to Jonathan had reinforced his personal practice, something that came first in his life. All else came after. "If you think I can't commit because I never married, I want to know. I'm eager to be in a loving relationship with a partner and I'll commit completely if I find the right one."

As I leaned in toward him over the small table between us, I studied his face, his hands, and empathically tuned in. His words were sincere. I suspected that my inner guidance had brought me to a soul mate, and realized that it is never too late to open one's heart to love again.

As we talked, we discovered how many times we'd been brought into close proximity over the decades. I'd almost bought a home just two doors away from him, while on a trip with my late husband. We'd both lived in Florida and before this, in Colorado, at the same time. We had traveled in circles that had not intersected, only bounced against each other, until now.

I was cautious about making a mistake, and as we continued to meet and I learned more about him my concerns lessened. We found that our tastes were alike in most every way, and our personal choices mirrored each other. The same toothbrush, the same little flashlight on our key chains, and more. We enjoyed one another's company for the next fourteen months, settling into a pattern of meditating together at the local Sangha every Tuesday evening, and sharing our weekends together. He brought sincerity, humor, a love of simple things, mutual joy in art and music, and for me, a new circle of friends. Our relationship, so comfortable and loving, deepened further, and we continue to live a blissful life together. My years of celibacy had much to teach me, but I was happy to end that period and live a full life again with my new love.

> I will repay you for the years the locusts have eaten---the great locust and the young locust, the other locusts and the locust swarm --- my great army that I sent among you, You will have plenty to eat, until you are full, and you will praise the name of the Lord your God, who has worked wonders for you. (Joel 2:25-26)

Jonathan and I are alike in our creativity, independence, and spirituality. This led to a special blessing for us. When a revered avatar, Sri Amma Karunamayi, left India to tour America, we traveled to be with her in a day of meditation. What a blessing it was to be lifted up in meditation with someone who has been in Divine Union for over thirty years! Before our day of retreat with her, she met with and blessed her hundreds of devotees, and we were among them. As we waited for our moment alone with her, Jonathan whispered, "Why don't we ask her to bless our union?" And so we went up to her as a couple, holding in our hearts our intentions to be together until our lives end, and passing our written commitments to her, she read them and prayed. Then she laid her hands on our heads. The energy of her holy intentions passed into us. We've since had ample evidence of how much and how beautifully our union was blessed.

In the years that have passed since then, I feel safe and at peace, understood and encouraged. I am appreciated and adored, both when I stumble and when I soar. I have been given all that I had imagined in prior years, when I longed for more. All that has come to pass for me has occurred because I have let go of my sense-driven intellect, listened to the Holy Spirit within me, and obeyed. My unswerving desire to reunite with Source, while back in my body, has led to the beginnings of wisdom, and a heart filled with a love passing into me and out to the Universe.

To paraphrase a passage in James 3:3-12, if you put a bit into the mouth of a horse to make it obey you, you can turn the whole animal. Or take a ship as an example. Although large and driven by strong winds, it is steered by a very small rudder wherever the pilot wants it to go. Likewise, the tongue which is a small part of the body will steer one's outcomes. Like the spoken word, the persistent thoughts of the mind and one's inner visions will drive outcomes. The words and the visions become beautiful when one aligns the personal will with Divine will by listening closely and trusting.

I stand strong in seeing all things working for good and that all will be even better than I can imagine. Now my internal workings and my manifestations as a human are closer to the eternal truth of love than ever before. I *see* joy, peace, wisdom, knowledge, and overarching love, and it is so, just as it is in Heaven. I know that Spirit lives within me, and within you.

Learning to consciously create is a gift beyond all imagining, for this child, now no longer even maiden but now a crone, who knew nothing of this and once created total chaos out of ignorance. There is no greater joy than to live as one of the One's creations, embodying love as a human in this laboratory for growth we call Earth. I know that the greatest law of life, the law of love, is infinite kindness, and I am grateful for all that has occurred for it has led me to embody, in my own imperfect way, all that it is.

I remain one with the One, while in a body. It is after all, just me and God, and it is all joy, whether within or outside of a body, if one only cherishes and nurtures the connection to Our Source, Love Itself.

III

REFLECTIONS FOR YOU

2020

The energy of the Primal Will courses through me. It breaks down every obstacle to its onward movement. It opens my understanding so that I perceive the beauty of the great pattern of manifestation. The One Identity transforms me into Its likeness and opens my eyes to the wonders of Its Perfect Law. eje

THIS IS NOT A STORY OF "WOMAN TRIUMPHS over adversity" but a paean to the glory of life in a body where we have, by free will, the opportunity to channel all the good of Our Source. It is my song of joy and thanksgiving, written for you and Our Source. The challenges of my life were a gift, for they led to the pivotal moment when I sought God with all my heart, mind, and soul. I did not anticipate that this act would lift my personal burdens away, but it did indeed restore me to wholeness in mind, body and spirit. Because of my willingness to turn my heart toward the Light, I was restored in every way. Yes, I willingly focused all of my attention upon this Light, but then I found that it was not my little self but rather that greater Self that opened my heart to All That Is, through grace.

The glory of the eternal nature! The goodness, love, power, knowledge, holy union in relationship with all aspects of creation (for this is how we love Ourselves). . . there is so much to be joyful for in life! May you see that God is everywhere and everything---see It in yourself and others!

I hold such love for you, my reader, or I would not have written this book. I have also held great love for my own unique being, knowing that I have been created like none other, and that all I have lived has been for the good pleasure of the One. It brings me great pleasure to recognize how the Holy Spirit within us all has created through me, and my little self has learned to listen and obey, leading to ever greater bliss. I offer my personal story to you, lending proof that doing this — seeking only God and nothing else — will transform and heal all areas of your life no matter how extreme the circumstances may be.

I have learned in the doing that metaphysics and science are converging, and that my inner guides and teachers and my own Higher Self have led me to understand enough of both to heal on all levels. As the ancients who carried forward the mystery school tradition knew, the manifestations we perceive as reality occur based on their environment — that vibrational field of emotion and desire and fear. Further, that manifestations can be dynamically changed based on our personal will and focus. Both science and spirit agree that there is a unified field of energy which is equally capable of wave or particle, and that it will take whatever form, or not, based on our viewing of it. All is malleable and yields to our beliefs. We are both unconscious and conscious creators, and our life experiences are manifestations of our strongest beliefs.

When I cried out to Source, "Reveal Yourself," I believe that it changed my inner vision first at a spiritual level, then at the physical level, and lastly, at the level of the mind.

I was then blessed to have been taught, not by Earthly instructors, but through the unseen yet real guidance one perceives through the heart, in the spaciousness of meditation. It was only later that I learned the words to describe my experience through reading the words of others, as I continued to test and experiment as inner guidance led me to. I was encouraged to become a conscious co-creator of my life, and this changed everything.

Life always met my expectations, for reality was always just as I saw it. This is worth pondering. . . I was a victim when I saw myself to be one. I was empty, frightened, and defeated when I could see myself as nothing more than this. I see myself thriving in joy today, all of my desires thumping out into the Universal Substance like a homing device, giving me a life of abundance, joy, fulfillment, peace, love, and an eternal assurance of security. And it is just as I now see it, in my mind's eye, or *even better* than I'm able to see with my limited mortal envisioning. I am free to do this without impedance, thanks to grace.

I am surely blessed to know from experiences outside of my body during meditations as well as my near death experience that this Earthly life is but a freeze frame, slow motion play in which I am free to make exactly the mistakes that I've made, and to stumble onto life-changing discoveries, as well. Perhaps you already knew these things! In that case, I'm certain you feel joy in knowing that one more soul has found her way Home, though still in a body, in this far away slow vibration we call Earth.

An even greater truth to life, as I now see it, is this: There is something beyond intellect and application of will, which is magical, and it is to be approached with humility, with reverence and awe, for it is energy from on High, that beautiful influx of grace that comforts and clears the way, a greater will to be surrendered to like a child to her protective and loving Father.

In my meditations, I glide into the One with a predicable trajectory: I begin with gratitude, and this transforms into praise, and in the act of praise I find that I am amidst the bliss of Our Source, my own Higher Self. Going beyond thought and personal feelings, there is only the glow and sound and feel of Divine Love. In this vibrational cloud of unknowing, I exist beyond time and space, just as I did when I was out of a body. Now in a body, one with the One, just me and God.

What my meditations teach me is this: We make life too complicated. It is simple. What we think about is formed first in the non-physical, and will materialize if we continue to *desire* it and believe that it will come to pass. Through clear prayer (as if your declaration is already manifest) and dialogue with God in all of His and Her forms your highest and truest heart desires will become clear, and as you continue to speak from your heart to God with honesty and humility, the path will continue to light up before you.

True desire is accompanied by emotion and feeling. Because desire is anything you dwell on with feeling, "desires" can also be the aggregation of emotion and repetitive thoughts of things that we do not want----things that we fear, dread, worry over, or otherwise view as caution signs on the highways of our lives. Connect to your Higher Self, that part of you that God has conceived from the beginning, to move closer to the light of your highest desires.

That which we are focusing on might manifest as bad dreams coming true, or endless detours which prevent us from reaching a happy destination. It is possible to dwell in the land of failure, until we discover for ourselves that our thoughts and feelings are momentary blockages and can be changed. Every second of time can be a new beginning! All of life is vibration. Choose your vibration, and you change the geography of the road you are traveling toward that dream destination that you feel will bring you the most joy. Recall that all good things come from the Father, who loves you. Humble yourself, get out of your own way, don't try to do it on your own without God.

Trust that you will be led. It is difficult to bog yourself down in worry and feelings of personal responsibility for outcomes. Instead, fill your mind with the promises of God, or with silent chants of the truth. How about "I am humble, and all good things come from the Father who loves me?" as a continuous stream of consciousness instead of negative mind chatter? The husband of my heart today, my dear Jonathan, has a similar way of doing this, and it may be a way that will resonate with you even more. He reminds himself always, "I and my Father are One. What my Father has, I have." Or, "I deserve happiness, and I am doing the right things, which create my happiness."

What you will then find is that simply traveling the road toward the destination is enough. There is joy in the creation of new things, even more so than enjoyment of that thing that has been created. For once we've received what we asked for, what we want then is not to sit back and enjoy that creation. . . what we want is to refine that, or replace that, and start over with something new! And so it really is as simple as it sounds: It is the journey not the destination in which quality of life is found.

Find joy in the moment no matter what. Put this above all else. Think about all the good things in your life, not the temporarily bad things. If it is in your heart to thank God for the good, do so. Dwell on the good, and keep releasing the negative thoughts when they arise. Road blocks will vanish, and fascinating new turns will appear on the road, and people and things will join you along the way, making the journey so much more enjoyable and easy. You will then experience loving camaraderie along the road.

> Be joyful always; pray continually; give thanks in all circumstances, for this is God's will for you in Christ Jesus. Do not put out the Spirit's fire; do not treat prophecies with contempt. Test everything. Hold on to the good.
> (I Thessalonians 5:16)

There are picnics and stops to play music and to sip wine and to watch the sunset together, and moments when you'll wish to snuggle down together and simply bask in each other's love, and to share each other's heart space and envision each other's deepest wishes. Those who enjoy traveling with you will remain with you, and those who do not will find a group more suitable to their leanings with which to travel.

When you look up into the heavens, and you see the stars twinkling overhead, what you see is an image of what once was, not what is. Likewise, with your creations. What you see around you now is your past, not your present. You are currently creating, and what actually is, is in process of emerging from the non-physical. It will soon appear before your eyes. What you see now is like the ancient broadcast of a star that is now perhaps extinguished. Do not put your trust in what you see with your physical eyes, but in what you see in your mind's eye.

Test this, and you will find that it is true. Try with something small, and something that you do not care too much about. Not caring a lot about the outcome will make the experiment more likely to manifest a quick result. If you don't attach too much angst to this, only just enough to feel curiosity and a sense of joy if the little experiment should succeed, that is enough effort. Don't set hard parameters to measure success either. Don't say that it has to happen within a certain timeframe, or that it has to look "just so," or that it has to come about in a specific way. Just hold a mental picture of the end result and sense what you'll be doing and feeling when it is manifest. Then let it go and let the non-physical power that creates Universes do the rest, to include its magical enhancements and upgrades to your little self's visions. You are meant to be joyful!

After you've had some successes with this light and fun approach to manifesting consciously, try something more important to you. Just imagine what it will be like when you experience that happy outcome. Keep looking, like Dorothy looking toward the Emerald City, at what lies ahead. Feel what it will be like to ride in the coach, pulled along behind the beautifully strong haunches and draping wisps of the horses' tails before you, through the emerald streets lined with cheering residents, all happy that you've arrived. Think of this rather than how you will travel to the city. Be in the city now and feel and see and touch and taste and smell and sense all the nuances of that place. Your manifestations will arrive in magical ways through synchronicities, as quickly as you ignore the road signs of doubt and discouragement. Now, let this go, and let it happen. Enjoy yourself in the present moment, the future moment when it happens, and then remain in this state when you conceive your next desire.

You are capable of creating, or manifesting, anything, and I mean anything, that you desire. You are capable of shedding unhelpful programming and mind ruts that cause you to repeat unpleasant experiences. You'll be given tools, perhaps like I was, or you may be blessed with an instant healing. You are yourself, like the manifestations you see before your eyes, as malleable as the things you bring out into the physical, and the rapidity of your change is, at least in part, up to you. You'll be led to your own tools, your own truth, your own self-actualization, in your own way when you learn to "die daily."

We are all loved so very much. The Universe is designed for us to succeed. Once this Earthly life is complete, you shall see that the roadblocks were insignificant, and that you have achieved a great deal. You will take away, with joy, all the experiences you've acquired about the art of consciously creating. I believe that you will be refining this ability here in future Earth incarnations, or maybe you'll decide to take this skill and apply it elsewhere in this limitless Universe.

We are united, one with the One in spirit, now and always. We are in fact, It, in a brave lower register of vibration, where time and space force us to slow down and experience each step of the creative process. This slowness also gives us time to correct what appear to us to be personal mistakes. In fact, there are no mistakes in an existence that is eternal, and in which we are in constant vibration or motion. Is the top of the sine wave more correct than the bottom of it? No. This is a world of contrast which we refer to as duality, and the up-beat is no more correct than the down-beat of the metronome. It is in the contrast that you discover what you truly desire. And it is this that drives you toward those emerald cities of your own imagination.

Stop thinking and planning and for a while just talk to God in private. You will often see a trail light up, a path that leads to greater joy.

Becoming quiet is the key to learning and upward movement. Meditation will lead you to deep inner guidance. If you choose not to act upon the inner wisdom you receive, or feel that you are unable to, please do not think less of yourself. You are still keeping the channel of love open by meditating.

Then you will find that the lifeblood of love cannot continue flowing into and through you, unless you are willing to forgive. You will be given, I trust, the ways and means to do this just like I was, if you are sincere and ready for Divine intervention. It will be a constant question that you must ask: Do I hold animosity toward anyone or anything? Through this daily questioning, this daily self-examination, you will identify and then can clear any obstructions which exist within you.

At the level of Higher Self while in meditation, you will know that you are always safe, unharmed by anything that might appear to harm you in your temporal existence, and will not ascribe your problems to others. This level of awareness that all is eternally well is apparent immediately to those who pass temporarily to the other side during a near death experience. Those who return will attest to their abrupt awareness that they went Home where all is safe and well. They have a sense of relief that they no longer are confined by a body, and no longer deluded into believing death is the ultimate harm that can come to an individual. They realize that death, like all else less than this in terms of insults to the body or mind, are temporary experiences that are quick sensations that, within the greater scope of experience, hardly even register as being significant. And that there is nothing but love when one is beyond time and space.

In eternity, there is no measurement of time, so if a goal is not accomplished by the expiration of a manmade deadline, it is of no consequence. There will be other opportunities. It is best to approach all personal growth with this attitude. You will eventually want to grow more, and growth will occur at the time that is most advantageous for your success. We grow in stages, adjusting to new perceptions and behaviors gradually. When you become comfortable, it will begin to again press upon you: What is the right thing to try now? What is upon my heart to do? And the next step of growth will begin.

There will never be a time that you will not wish to grow. The motion will never stop, but you will become ever more attuned to the nuances of this. You will delight in the slightest shift in perspective, for these shifts reveal the glint of the facets of the jewel of which you are a part. The slightest shift in perspective will reveal beauty, as if for the first time, and you will continue to shift, along with all other aspects of creation that are also in the undulating movement of eternity. Every shift is for the good, as you'll in time see, but when things seem unclear, trust and continue in faith, believing. This attitude is like resting in the eternal arms of love, in the midst of change. Dismiss your inner critic's whisperings that you are flawed and mistake-prone, for this isn't so. You are eternally right and good, and Source Itself takes great joy in every moment, even those you may criticize yourself for, and it is broadcasting Its immeasurable love to all of its creations, including you, unconditionally.

Within a body, your sensations are limited to it, your feelings are limited to it, and your thoughts seem contained within it. Your spiritual highs and lows feel as if they are also contained within your skin, and that no one else sees inside your unique mental and emotional space, or feels the sensory inputs of your body. But this is not true. Within the non-physical of your internal "mind" or "soul" world I have just described, you are never alone. Trust that there are unseen forces dedicated to holding the vibrations necessary to uplift and to sustain you. Like separate notes in a beautiful symphony of vibrations that make up existence, these beautiful vibrations were created to sustain mankind, and are called by some, angels. Led by the creative force Herself, if you meditate upon this Divine Feminine, this nurturing and all-forgiving advocate, you may begin to feel Her, too. If you feel alone, ask for evidence that you are not. You shall receive it.

When meditation beckons you back home again and again, you may find that the bliss of Heaven extends into the periods in between your sessions. Your heart will say that "all is well" and resonate with the assurance that you are loved and you are never alone. And that this verity applies not just to you, but to those who, unlike you, are unaware. It is available but never forced upon anyone, for it is accessed only when you turn your will and desire toward it. The unaware are benefiting equally, although their eyes haven't yet been opened to see that this is happening. We are, every one of us, being led unawares, with constant nurturing beaming down equally upon all of creation. We're all being led to our awakening, one at a time, at our own pace. The same undifferentiated light and love will continue to shower down for eternity. All the plants in the garden are receiving the light. Some will thrive. Others won't, but all is still eternal and nothing is lost.

Some imagine a future in which they shall no longer exist, having either no belief in their eternal nature, or alternatively believing that who "we" are simply disappears in a merger with the undefined and un-manifest light. Experience tells me that neither is true. It seems that the point of our apparent separation into unique entities or souls is to amplify the depth of experience and beauty of the Whole, and we were made for Its pleasure. We are made of and move within this ineffable Whole. It is possible that creation shall shift in a way that we are no longer recognizable in the form we now take, but as uniquely evolving beings, we are eternal. As above, so below. The macrocosm and the microcosm reflect each other in beauty, and if we can think of this Whole as a diamond, then consider that every facet of this diamond is precious.

When we begin to awaken, we long to return to Source. But it is actually like a tractor beam drawing you upwards, causing you to evolve and grow into the ability to live at this higher altitude. The energy comes from above. Source echoes your cries for union, saying, "We are love, and we love you." You are made of love, by love, and for love. Look at the baby's demeanor, for it has a mature soul that has just left the non-physical and re-entered our physical world. See its joy? See how it has an awareness of bodily sensations and that this also brings joy? See its ability to focus its eyes upon yours, and you see eternity as you drop into the velvety pools of light emanating from them? You will not see anything but light and love and joy when you look into those eyes. Babies are the reminders to those of you who have lost track of the light from which you were yourself made. And the joy they take in their newly created bodies should be an inspiration to you as well.

You were perfectly formed for your plans in this body of yours. But there comes a natural moment in time, when you shall leave it for Home. Death is a beautiful, comfortable opening to the fullness of who you are and a revelation of who God is. You remain alive, body or not. Your heavenly Father/Mother has created you, and there is none other like you for all eternity. At every stage of your eternal movement, the Father/Mother God continues to love you boundlessly, for you were their creation at first, but now you are your own. Our Creator is achieving endless and ever expanding joy through each of us, Its creations. This is the secret, mystical truth within the dogma and jargon and ritual and practices that all religions on Earth share.

Hearing my personal story, it is fair for you to ask: If the soul heals, will the body? Not always. Your physical body's blueprint, conceived by all that is good and pure joy, is perfect, but is willing to take upon itself the burdens of misunderstanding, if the mind and emotional body cannot. It has been designed to be this way. Sometimes the body might be too far gone to reverse through one's prayers, or the mind might be too far gone to pray. It can be appealing to instead, simply yield to the pull that returns us to Heaven. In my own case, I came very close to this point more than once. Sometimes there is purpose in surviving, although in suffering. If it has not become clear regarding suffering, may I say that the body, taking upon itself burdens your mind cannot handle, might allow your soul to remain alive in our slow motion interactions with others, instead of fleeing from the Earth experience at the first seeming insult or hurt that this life presents to you? And that continued suffering will cause you to cry out for answers and for connection? If it is possible to progress without suffering, I have not experienced this myself, so cannot speak of any other way.

When I look about me, I observe that we all seem to "choose" our own path of suffering. Certainly not always at a conscious level but we take suggestions unaware, from our Higher Self. May I suggest that we choose this path of suffering in order to grow? There is so much suffering in this world, how could I have the nerve to tell you this! Some say they would have given up and died if they'd been forced to endure my path, but to me it was exactly what was needed to fully learn that I'm right to trust, like the child of a loving parent, that I am unconditionally adored and that all works out for good. In this perspective, when I look at those around me, I feel many suffer

235

more than I ever have, and I pray always for the Highest Good to come quickly for us all.

I struggled so much in my life to understand Jesus' daily prayer. What does "Thy will be done" now mean to me? It means to be humble, meek, trusting, or surrendered (whatever of these words means the most to you), to a Father that knows my needs and is bringing only His goodness to me in ways that may seem mysterious or even heartless, but prove to expand my capacity for love and joy. Being surrendered, I find that I am detached from outcomes (even pain and death), although I willfully focus my thoughts and feelings on beautiful visualizations of all that is put on my heart as desires. It is a paradox that I no longer try to understand. Simply, it is the way of love.

For me, I was surrendered first by physical limitations. I was surrendered by biology, really, when I returned to Earth in a right-brained state that kept my soul in Heaven although tied to a broken body. When my soul fully landed back here on Earth and I could do nothing else, I surrendered by conscious choice. Now I surrender daily and talk to my Father/Mother like a begging child that I'll remain an open channel for my own Higher Self to live through me.

What I agreed to proceed with in the summer of 1995 healed me on all levels. It took about seventeen years to complete, and gosh yes, there was suffering involved. But, as it is said in traditional Christian circles, I was lost and now I am found. I now appreciate the lovely nuances of the mental, physical, and spiritual motion within me. I see myself to be a tiny inlet fed by the

> But we have this treasure in jars of clay to show that this all-surpassing power is from God and not from us. We are hard pressed on every side, but not crushed; perplexed, but not in despair; persecuted, but not abandoned; struck down, but not destroyed.
> (2 Corinthians 4:7-9)

infinite ocean of Love Itself. I understand how the waves are created within my inlet, and the draw of the tide into the great ocean itself. In that sense, I am consciously one with the One. Was this not worth some momentary suffering?

This body of mine remains imperfect, and I find this to be a spur for continued growth. Some of my personal visions have not yet materialized. I have often wondered why they do not manifest according to the time table I think that they should. Over time I have come to realize that the incomplete, the imperfect, is what compels me to try harder to align my will with God's. It is what reminds me that it is not little me who does the work. Incongruence has been one of my more subtle teachers, and I am grateful for this. We are never finished, and the lesson I see is that suffering continues to drive me closer to Source while here in a body.

My progression from dis-ease to wellness was the perfect means to meekness, and then awe, when I asked for and received the immense love of Heaven while still in a body. I am grateful beyond words for the grace that gives me the feeling that I am Home whether in Heaven or on Earth. I *know* that we are eternal and we are loved. I know this, not because I was taught this by others, but because I embarked on a difficult journey from life to death and back to life again, not once but twice, and learned it for myself.

Offered in all humility,

Emily Jean

Recommended Reading

Anatomy of the Spirit: The Seven Stages of Power and Healing; Caroline Myss, Ph.D., 1996

Angelspeake, A Guide: How to Talk with Your Angels; Barbara Mark and Trudy Griswold, 1995

Angels in My Hair; Lorna Byrne, 2008

The Art of Being and Becoming; Hazrat Inayat Khan, 1982, 1989, 2005

The Bach Remedies Workbook: A Study Course in the Bach Flower Remedies; Stefan Ball; 2005

The Brain That Changes Itself: Stories of Personal Triumph from the Frontiers of Brain Science; Norman Doidge, M.D., 2007

The Body Never Lies: The Lingering Effects of Hurtful Parenting; Alice Miller, 2006

The Charles Fillmore Collection; Charles Fillmore, dates vary by volume within the collection

Clarifying the Natural State: A Principal Guidance Manual for Mahamudra; Dakpo Tashi Namgyal (1512-1587), foreward by Khenchen Thrangu Rinpoche, 2001

The Cloud upon the Sanctuary; Karl von Eckartshausen, forward by
Edward Dunning, 2003

The Complete James Allen Collection; James Allen, Manor Books
2017, originally written between 1901 and 1919

Complete Works of H. Emilie Cady (Annotated), H. Emilie Cady,
introduction by Russell A. Kemp, by Unity Village Press, first
printed in 1896 in *Lessons in Truth* and articles within *Unity
Magazine*

The Concise Yoga Vasistha; Swami Venkatesananda, 1984

Courageous Dreaming: How Shamans Dream the World Into Being;
Alberto Villoldo, Ph.D., 2008

Coyote Healing: Miracles in Native Medicine; Lewis Mehl-Madrona,
M.D., Ph.D., 2003

*The Creation of Health: The Emotional, Psychological, and Spiritual
Responses That Promote Health and Healing;* Caroline Myss,
Ph.D., C. Norman Shealy, M.D., 1988, 1993

*Creative Visualization: Using the Power of Your Imagination to Create
What You Want in Your Life;* Shakti Gawain, 1978, 1995, 2002

*The Death of Religion and the Rebirth of Spirit: A Return to the
Intelligence of the Heart;* Joseph Chilton Pearce, 2007

The Divine Romance: Tales of an Unearthly Love; John Davidson,
2004

*Energy Medicine: Balancing Your Body's Energies for Optimal Health,
Joy and Vitality;* Donna Eden with David Feinstein, Ph.D.,
Foreword by Caroline Myss, 1998, 2008

The EFT Manual; Gary Craig, 2010, 2011

The Empath's Survivor Guide: Life Strategies for Sensitive People;
Judith Orloff, 2017

Entering the Castle: An Inner Path to God and Your Soul; Caroline
Myss, 2007

*The Essential Rabbi Nachman: Teachings and Stories for All on Faith,
Hope and Joy;* Avraham Greenbaum, 2016

The Face Before I Was Born: A Spiritual Autobiography; Llewellyn
Vaughan-Lee, 1998

Feelings Buried Alive Never Die. . .; Karol K. Truman, 1991, 2003, 2010

Fragments of a Love Story: Reflections on the Life of a Mystic; Llewellyn Vaughan-Lee, 2011

The Gnostic Gospels: Including The Gospel of Judas, The Gospel of Thomas, The Gospel of Mary Magdalene; Alan Jacobs, 2006, 2007, 2008

Healing Words: The Power of Prayer and The Practice of Medicine, Larry Dossey, M.D., 1993

The Heart of Centering Prayer: Nondual Christianity in Theory and Practice; Cynthia Bourgeault, 2016

The HeartMath Solution; Doc Childre and Howard Martin, 1999

The Hero with a Thousand Faces; Joseph Campbell, 1949, 1968, 2008

The Hidden Gospel: Decoding the Spiritual Message of the Aramaic Jesus; Neil Douglas-Klotz, 1999

Highly Intuitive People: 7 Right-Brain Traits to Change the Lives of Intuitive-Sensitive People; Heidi Sawyer, 2015

Holy Spirit (Boundless Energy of God); Ron Roth, Ph.D. with Peter Occhiogrosso, 2000

Inner Work: Using Dreams and Active Imagination for Personal Growth; Robert A. Johnson, 2009

The Intelligent Heart: Transform Your Life with the Laws of Love; David McArthur and Bruce McArthur, 1997

Interior Castle; St. Teresa of Avila, translated by E. Allison Peers, 2008

Invisible Acts of Power: Channeling Grace in Your Everyday Life; Caroline Myss, 2004

Jung's Map of the Soul: An Introduction; Murray Stein, 1998, 12th printing 2010

The Kybalion: Hermetic Philosophy; The Three Initiates, 1912, 1940

The Law of Attraction: The Basics of the Teachings of Abraham; Esther and Jerry Hicks, 2006

Lord, Teach Us to Pray; Rev. Andrew Murray, 1896

Meister Eckhart: Selections from His Essential Writings, Foreword by John O'Donohue; Harper Collins Spiritual Classics, 1981

Metaphysical Bible Dictionary; Unity School of Christianity, 1931

Mind Over Medicine: Scientific Proof That You Can Heal Yourself; Lissa Rankin, M.D., 2013

Mind to Matter: The Astonishing Science of How Your Brain Creates Material Reality; Dawson Church, Ph.D., 2018

The Miracle of Metaphysical Healing; Evelyn M. Monahan, 1975

The Perennial Philosophy; Aldous Huxley, 1944, 1945, 1990, 2004, 2009

Perfect Health: The Complete Mind Body Guide; Deepak Chopra, M.D., 1991, 2000

The Physics of Angels: Exploring the Realm Where Science and Spirit Meet; Matthew Fox and Rupert Sheldrake, 1996, 2014

The Power of Infinite Love and Gratitude: An Evolutionary Journey to Awakening Your Spirit; Dr. Darren R. Weissman, 2005

Power Prayer: A Program for Unlocking Your Spiritual Strength; Gary and Chrissie Blaze, 2012

Power Through Constructive Thinking; Emmet Fox, HarperCollins e-books

Practical Mysticism: A Little Book for Normal People; Evelyn Underhill, 1915, now in public domain

The Practice of the Presence of God; Brother Lawrence, now in public domain

Radical Remission: The Nine Key Factors That Can Make a Real Difference; Kelly A. Turner, Ph.D., 2014

Reclaiming the Bible for a Non-Religious World; Bishop John Shelby Spong, 2011

Rosemary Gladstar's Herbal Recipes for Vibrant Health; Rosemary Gladstar, 2001, 2008

St. John of the Cross: Dark Night of the Soul; Dover Thrift Editions, 2003

The Science of Mind; Ernest Holmes, 2007

Secrets of the Lost Mode of Prayer: The Hidden Power of Beauty, Blessing, Wisdom, and Hurt; Gregg Braden, 2006

Seven Masters, One Path: Meditation Secrets from the World's Greatest Teachers; John Selby, 2003

The Song of Songs: The Soul and the Divine Beloved; John Davidson, 2004

The Spiritual Teaching of Ramana Maharshi, Foreword by C.G. Jung; Shambhala Dragon Edition, 1988

Spontaneous Evolution: Our Positive Future (and a Way to Get There from Here); Bruce H Lipton, Ph.D., and Steve Bhaerman, 2009

The Spontaneous Healing of Belief: Shattering the Paradigm of False Limits; Gregg Braden, 2008

The Sufi Path of Love: The Spiritual Teachings of Rumi; William C. Chittick, 1983

The Tarot: A Key to the Wisdom of the Ages; Paul Foster Case, 1947, 1990, 2006

Things Hidden: Scripture as Spirituality; Richard Rohr, 2008

Twelve World Teachers: A Summary of their Lives and Teachings; Manly P. Hall, 1965

Unconditional Love and Forgiveness; Edith R. Stauffer, Ph.D., 1987

Under the Table & How to Get Up: Jewish Pathways of Spiritual Growth; Avraham Greenbaum, 1991

The Universal Dream Key: The 12 Most Common Dream Themes Around the World; Patricia Garfield, Ph.D., 2001

Walking Meditation, Nguyen Anh-Huong and Thich Nhat Hanh, 2006

Whispers From Eternity; Paramahansa Yogananda, 1935, 1958, 1959, 1973

Why Love Matters: How Affection Shapes a Baby's Brain; Sue Gerhardt, 2004

You Can Heal Your Life; Louise L. Hay, 1999

Acknowledgments

It is tempting to thank everyone I have ever met, but I shall limit this to the people instrumental in bringing this manuscript to publication.

Thank you, Reverend C, for encouraging me to write my story for the benefit of others.

Thank you my dearest partner, Jonathan N., for the discipline and love you offered as I persisted in writing what was, for me, a painful look back in order to illustrate a before and after picture for my readers. I thank you, Jonathan, for the many occasions when you listened to early drafts being read to you, and for your eagle eye in spotting errors that would detract from an easy read for others.

Thank you to my additional early readers, Gay, Ken, and Colette for your suggestions on how to make this easy and informative for others no matter the background or orientation. Lastly, thanks to Cat for her encouragement and her lovely cello practice as I wrote Part III.

About the Author

Emily Jean Entwistle was once a successful executive until a brain stem stroke and blood cancer at forty-three took her on a twenty-four year journey. Now, sixty-seven, Entwistle shares life with her love, Jonathan, and their sweet little cat. They divide their time between their home in the mountains and a primitive ranch in the wilderness.

Index

258

R

Rabbi Nachman 81, 240
Real 5, 20, 22, 26, 41, 42, 49, 50, 51, 101, 129, 140, 145, 155, 180, 184, 191, 225, 242
Reality (see also Real) xi, xiv, xvii, 2, 7, 85, 132, 133, 135, 136, 141, 142, 143, 146, 165, 180, 198, 225, 242
Reason xvii, 13, 16, 23, 24, 26, 44, 45, 59, 73, 84, 109, 161, 168, 179, 191, 196, 215
Reincarnation (see also Incarnation) 150
Relationships 8, 22, 25, 28, 35, 37, 40, 65, 67, 70, 104, 149, 163, 189, 218, 219, 224
Religion (see also Theology) 115, 240
Remission 178, 194, 195, 242
Review 23, 25, 27, 39
Right brain xiii, 39, 40
Ripple(s) v, xii, xiii, xiv, xv, xvi, xix, 8, 14, 15, 25, 26, 29, 31, 42, 44, 45, 49, 50, 51, 54, 55, 57, 59, 62, 69, 74, 79, 80, 81, 84, 87, 94, 96, 98, 99, 100, 101, 102, 103, 104, 105, 106, 108, 115, 116, 117, 119, 120, 122, 123, 124, 125, 127, 128, 132, 135, 139, 141, 143, 145, 146, 150, 151, 153, 157, 158, 163, 164, 166, 167, 168, 169, 170, 175, 176, 178, 179, 181, 182, 184, 186, 190, 192, 193, 194, 195, 196, 198, 199, 200, 201, 202, 203, 204, 205, 206, 207, 208, 211, 212, 213, 214, 215, 218, 220, 225, 228, 229, 232, 234, 235, 237, 240, 241, 242, 243
Rosary (see also Rosary Beads) 214
Rudraksha Mala 214

S

Sabotage 174
Salutation of the Sun 116
Samadhi 68, 81, 115, 120, 176
Sayer Ji 182
Script 51
Secret(s) v, xii, xiii, xiv, xv, xvi, xix, 8, 14, 15, 25, 26, 29, 31, 42, 44, 45, 49, 50, 51, 54, 55, 57, 59, 62, 69, 74, 79, 80, 81, 84, 87, 94, 96, 98, 99, 100, 101, 102, 103, 104, 105, 106, 108, 115, 116, 117, 119, 120, 122, 123, 124, 125, 127, 128, 132, 135, 139, 141, 143, 145, 146, 150, 151, 153, 157, 158, 163, 164, 166, 167, 168, 169, 170, 175, 176, 178, 179, 181, 182, 184, 186, 190, 192, 193, 194, 195, 196, 198, 199, 200, 201, 202, 203, 204, 205, 206, 207, 208, 211, 212, 213, 214, 215, 218, 220, 225, 228, 229, 232, 234, 235, 237, 240, 241, 242, 243
See xi, xiii, xvi, xx, 7, 13, 15, 22, 27, 28, 29, 30, 38, 39, 44, 45, 54, 55, 58, 62, 74, 80, 90, 95, 98, 108, 118, 120, 121, 132, 133, 134, 140, 141, 146, 147, 157, 158, 162, 174, 178, 180, 192, 193, 195, 198,

Emily Jean Entwistle, a former executive and material girl with a mystical bent, was badly damaged by a childhood rife with sexual and psychological abuse. In one with the One, she shares a story of transformation because of a soul level agreement to evolve through suffering into wholeness and joy.

Entwistle chronicles her path to wholeness, offering details of her life. She was adopted into a frightening home and was a virtual prisoner until age eighteen. She was to die and go to heaven just when she reached tenuous stability as an adult. She returned from heaven, back to her broken body for the sake of another and was taught through service that the greatest law of life is love.

In this memoir, she tells how conscious communion with God can be experienced by anyone. While her story illustrates how this happened to her, it offers guidance on how others can experience this, too. Through her trials and triumphs, Entwistle has learned that we are eternal beings floating in a sea of love. Her journey from darkness to light teaches the truth that we are co-creators being led back, with the greatest love of all, to conscious communion with God.